T
OF
THE RED RIVER
GORGE

BY

DON F. FIG

Wordclay
3750 Priority Way South Drive, Suite 114
Indianapolis, IN 46240
www.wordclay.com

First published by Wordclay on 12/11/2007.
ISBN: 978-1-6048-1361-6 (sc)

Printed in the United States of America.

This book is printed on acid-free paper.

INTRODUCTION TO TALES

What the Golden Fleece was to Jason and his Argonauts so is the enticement of the Red River Gorge to visitors of Kentucky. Down through the ages, the lure of this land where spiritual renewal may be had for the asking, has intrigued visitors and local residents alike.

The following pages are a collection of tales of the Red River Gorge as told to me by old time residents of the area. Most interviews were in the 1960's and the majority of these locals have passed on. The significant fact of these tales beings to light the gorge is, and always has been, a special place. From the ancients who worshiped under the arches, to the current visitor seeking a regeneration of life through the transcendental of natural phenomenon.

Therefore, in a sense we have come full circle. The natural features of the gorge must have fascinated early man and are what brings visitors into the area today.
Commencing with the petroglyphs of the ancients, to interviews with old time residents who actually lived the story has been a rewarding endeavor.

Now, for your enlightenment, here are Tales of the Red River Gorge. I hope you enjoy reading as much as I take pleasure in presenting.

 Compiled at the Red River Gorge, Kentucky on January 30, 2002.

EARLY MAN IN THE RED RIVER GORGE

 Tales of the Red River Gorge is a collection of short stories of historical times, and petroglyphs from a prehistoric day as depicted by the carved symbols on rocks. Any time an attempt is made to decipher such things, you quickly pass from fact to a twilight world of inference in which we can say, "not this is true," but "only probably this is true". And from thence into a region of darkness, illuminated here and there by a guess, speculation or theory. We see through a glass, darkly. An interpretation of petroglyphs is certainly a guess. We have no way of knowing the reasoning or intent of the early authors and whether the carvings are art forms or communication. Therefore, any interpretation should be taken literally as an opinion and not as facts.

 The Red River Gorge has perhaps the largest concentration of petroglyps east of the Mississippi River. To have these many carvings in such a small area, indicates the Gorge was probably use as a setting for various ceremonies of the ancients. One of the most significant carvings is a symbolic man, women and child. Note the inverted "V" just above the scale representing the female. . Immediately above this is a stick-man representing the male. About midway to the right is the outline

6

of a child's foot. This probably depicts some special or important event.

There are many carvings that generate scant clues to the meaning of the symbols. Yet, if they are truly communication cryptograms, the message may be deciphered.

There are some reasons to believe the petroglyphs are communication devices rather than art. If a artistic expression was the original intent of the carver, it seems reasonable a smooth surface would have been selected. In fact, many smooth rock faces were often ignored in favor of uneven ones, leaving the impression the ancients were choosing a visible spot that could be easily located by someone else seeking a message. The exact reason for carving the petroglyphs is lost to history, but there is no doubt about the significant of these picture-writings, and the importance of vigorous protection of what remains. It has been many years since the valleys rang to the sharp sound of flint on stone as the ancient writer shaped his message, and the now forgotten trails felt the tread of his moccasined feet. Likewise, early humankind has disappeared along with the true meaning of the time when man first expressed his reasoning on the sandstone boulders.

It is unknown how many thousands of years ago man developed a spoken language.
Etymologists agree that sounds were developed long before humans learned to write the sounds by use of signs or symbols. In picture-writing (petroglyphs), drawings of objects are arranged to chronicle an event or some other thing important to the writer. These rock-writers apparently wanted their message to endure, cutting the grooves of their symbols sometimes an inch into the rock surface, then smoothed out the grooves by abrading. If you look in Genesis 11:1 there is a passage, which reads: "And the whole earth was of one language and one speech." Petroglyphs are in every quarter of the earth, and perhaps this may serve as a testimony that a written language was understood over the world.

The historical tales have at least some documented facts and many have been handed down for generations. Some can be traced through a Census, old photographs, and sometimes, early newspapers. The most rewarding is personal interviews with old time residents who actually lived the story. It is recognized that some inaccuracies may be present, but even so, there is no doubt about the historical significance and the need to preserve for future generations of those who visit the Red River Gorge

HE SLEEPY HOLLOW LODGE

Jack Sorrel, a local resident, completed the Sleepy Hollow Lodge in 1939. His name and date of construction is incised on the foundation of the house. Campbell Meekin, acting for the owners of the land (Mildred and Don Bishop) approached Sorrel with a proposal to build a hunting lodge or weekend retreat from "standard plans." Sorrel agreed and the structure was started in the fall of 1938.

The Bishop's were not local residents. They used the lodge for weekends away from the city. They sold the property in 1943 to Cecil Tyler, a Dayton, Ohio resident, who also used the area on weekends. Tyler sold to Boyd Newkirk, a local resident, in 1948 who added a small frame addition in 1949, and in 1970, the title passed to Hobart Moore, then to Tony Collins in 1972, Ralph Kittle in 1974 and finally secured in government ownership in 1994.

When Boyd Newkirk bought the cabin in 1948 he hung a wooden sign with routed letters on the porch beam proclaiming the "Sleepy Hollow Lodge." The sign stayed in place for many years finally disappearing around 1968, probably to a dorm room at some college campus.

The design of the lodge is reminisce of the Adirondack style of New York State and is by no means a native Kentucky habitat copy.

EARLY INHABITANTS OF THE RED RIVER

When the hunters of the Paleo-Indian culture arrived in the Red River Valley about 10,000 years ago, the environment was substantially different from now. The Pleistocene glacier advances were ending but it would be some time before conditions similar to those of today would prevail. Although the Pleistocene Glacier never penetrated the Red River Gorge (stopping within 200 miles), the effects were far reaching. The climate became considerable cooler, but was not severe enough to displace the existing vegetation. This permitted the infiltration of a few far northern species, which remain to this day in relic niches.

Due to this extenuating glacier effect the gorge provides an ultra-protected habitat. The coolness has favored the persistence of northern type plants, and the depth and orientation have given southern species protection against the rigors of winter. Northern and southern plant species may be found growing side by side.

The prehistory of the Red River Valley covers a time span of approximately 10,000 years. Within this scheme, the cultural sequence is divided into four "traditions" or cultural configurations:

1.   Paleo-Indian – (13000-8000 B.C.) Hunters, small bands, fluted projectile points.
2.   Archaic – (8000-1000 B.C.) Gatherers, first substantial evidence of human occupation in gorge, stemmed and notched projectile points, scraping and piercing implements made of chert and bone. Appearance of flint axes, atlatl, and implements of ground stone for food processing. Rockshelter and bottomland sites were both utilized during this period.

3.   Woodland – (1000 B.C. -900 A.D.) Marked by the appearance of three

significant innovations; the introduction of pottery and horticulture,

mortuary ceremonialism, and projectile points stemmed and notched.

4.   Fort Ancient – (900 A.D. – 1700) Projectile points were small and triangular in shape. People lived in bottomland sites and rock shelters and were hunters and farmers.

The importance of the archeological resources of the Red River Valley is well established. Their historic, cultural, scientific and social significance is tremendous.

Many of these resources have been severely damaged or destroyed. The remainder must be vigorously protected.

LOG BRANDS OF THE RED RIVER GORGE

Like cattle brands in the old west, Red River Gorge logs were also branded to identify the various logging companies active in the late 1800's. Log Brands were registered and recorded similar to cattle brands. When the logs were splashed on the spring tides log booms caught them. The branded logs, identified by the owner when they were tallied, were much like a cattle roundup. Just as cattle brands were altered by rustlers, the same problem existed among loggers. Log rustlers removed logs from the stream before they reached the log booms. The original brand was sawn off the butt end in a thin slice. The rustler's brand was stamped on the freshly cut surface. This was known as "dehorning." It must have been a common practice at that time since laws were passed prohibiting defacing or removal of brands.

The branding was done with a branding hammer made up by the registered owner with the symbol used to stamp the logs in relief. One of the earliest registered brands in the Gorge was:

Red River Lumber Company, adopted 1889 and registered by W. C. Pryor

13

It has been many years since the Red River rang to the sound of branding hammers striking the logs and the now forgotten trails felt the tread of the logger's feet. Likewise, the art of dehorning has vanished along with the log booms, splash dams and dinky engines.

The day of the old time log brander (and dehorner) has gone the way of the Great Auk and Passenger Pigeon.

A SPLASH DAM PRIMER

 Splash dams were once quite common throughout the drainages of the Red River Gorge, and were used extensively during the logging boom of the late 1800's and early 1900's. A model at the Gladie Creek Historic Site shows the basic structure and design of one such dam.

The Red River is a unique mountain stream located between the Licking and Kentucky Rivers. It has three forks, north, south and middle. The north fork is the principal stream; it originates at the foot of Town Flats, corners of Wolfe, Morgan, Magoffin and Breathitt counties. Meandering through the rolling countryside of Hazel Green as a calm and peaceful stream, the river plunges into a cliff-studded gorge and winds its way for nine tortuous miles of perpendicular canyons before breaking back into civilization at just below sky Bridge. After leaving the canyons, the river becomes calm and peaceful again before flowing into the Kentucky River near Boonsboro.

The tributaries of the Red are relatively small, Gladie and Copperas Creek being the longest streams. However, the watercourses were the most economical way to move logs out of the Red River Gorge. Roads in the area were few and poor. Splash dams provided the logical solution for increasing the water flow. By building dams on smaller streams, the impounded water could be released through a triggered gate flushing the logs out.

Logging during this era was quite strenuous and required getting the standing timber down and somehow, some way, getting the logs to a mill. A typical way was by dragging the logs by mule, horse or oxen to the smaller tributaries located throughout the area. The tributaries were blocked with splash

15

dams to hold back water until the spring drive. When sufficient water was pooled, the dam gate was opened by a pin or dynamited free, creating a loud "splash," thus allowing the logs to be carried down to the next dam where the process was repeated. The "splash" is what gave the "Splash dam" its name.

There were several types of dams used during this time. The crib-type dam, the post-type dam, the rafter-type dam, and of course dams that were simply blown apart when enough water was pooled. The crib-type was the most permanent and expensive, lasting for four to sixteen years. The rafter-type lasted for one to two years, and the pile-type hardly lasted a year. Of course, the ones dynamited lasted for only one splash. The crib-type was the most used in the area. This was due to the amazing amount, and size, of trees in the area that it took a long time to log the Red River Gorge.

Basically the logs are released through the dam by knocking out a pin that holds a beam in place. The beam has several vertical fingers connected to it with horizontal planks positioned on the front of them. The cracks in the planks are sealed with clay or mud and are able to hold back the pooled water. When the pin is released, the fingers come loose releasing the planks and a torrent of water. The pin is the vital point and is tightly wedged between a post and the beam. It is released by taking a sledgehammer to it, for it is quite large and strong to be able back so much pressure.

The crib dam is a common form and is named thus because the buttress and wings are built of cribs usually filled with stone.

The foundation usually rests on bedrock and three parallel lines of large logs called "mud-sills" were placed across the stream from bank to bank. A cribwork was built up until it reached the level of the stream and a gate (sluiceway) was provided in the center of the stream through which the logs passed. Cost of such a structure varied from $1000 to $3000.

The rafter dam was cheaper to build than a crib dam and was useful where a large head of water was not required. Foundation and mudsills were similar to crib-type, In addition, the upstream face of the dam is angled.

The pile dam was a double row of piles driven to bedrock to form the buttress and wings. The space between the piles being filled with gravel and stone. This type, as far as known, was never used in the Red River Gorge.

The operation of the dams was a study in precision timing. The supervisor judged when conditions were ready to move the logs out of the area. Previously cut logs were stacked on the stream banks so that they could be released into the water quickly and easily. The stage was set for splashing after it had rained enough to raise the stream to a sufficient height. Word went out to the men that the splashing would start at a certain time. Bull crews armed with peaveys and other equipment waited along the streams to dump the logs into the rapidly flowing water, and to prod them along if they were stuck. The men at the dams were told when to release the splashes. The uppermost dam on the stream splashed first. Water levels at each downstream site were closely observed. When the men at these dams noticed an abrupt rise in the water level, they would trigger the gate. Timing was important as the rush of water and logs from the upper dams would destroy the lower dams if the gates were not opened in the right sequence.

Splashing continued in sequence on individual streams and simultaneously on other streams within the boundary of cut timber. The splashes generated a large tide by the time the logs reached the Red River. On occasion, logjams did occur despite the efforts of the bull crew. Doc Askins tells about one on Gladie Creek that was a mile long and he estimated involved between thirty-five and fifty thousand logs. The logs had to be blasted loose in this particular jam, although crews could usually find a key log that was holding the jam and by releasing it, free the rest of the logs.

For three or four decades surrounding the turn of the century, timber companies in eastern Kentucky used uniquely constructed splash dams to move timber from forest to mill. These dams are example of local ingenuity: They were designed to use local materials and be reusable. The roar of the rushing water and logs caused by splashing disappeared in the 1920's with the construction of roads into the Red River basin, ending an exciting and colorful period.

FIRST SETTLER IN RED RIVER GORGE

Nim Wills is credited with being the first white settler in the Gorge area. When he passed through the present day town of Campton, the only signs of habitation were old campfires where the courthouse now stands. According to stories handed down, Wills named the settlement Campton (for Camp Town) this is believed to be the site of John Swifts camp. The nearby creek, which runs through the town, was named Swift Camp Creek, but is usually referred to as Swift Creek.

There is a faint legend that Nim Wills outwitted a band of pursuing Indians near Tunnel Ridge, when he leaped over the side of a natural arch. Unbeknown to the Indians, there was a hidden ledge under the arch where Wills jumped and hid. The Indians thought he had plunged a hundred feet to the valley below. After their departure, Wills emerged from the covert ledge and stepped for home.

It is interesting to note the description of this arch knits well with the Arch of Triumph, located just off present day Tunnel Ridge Road.

THE BOATYARD

Near the confluence of Chimney Top Creek and the Red River is a long forgotten area known in times past as the "Boat Yard." It was in this area that Powell Rose around 1850, constructed barges from native White Oak; filled them with coal and floated down river to Clay City, Winchester, and sometimes even to Frankfort where he disposed of the entire load including the barge.

19

David Dale Owen made the following observation in 1857: "Near the mouth of Wolfe Pen Creek and Chimney Rock, the coal measure commence with 23 to 25 inch coal seam near their base...this bed has supplied coal for the Red River Forge and Rolling Mill."

HELL'S KITCHEN

About one ½ miles below Rock Bridge on Swift Camp Creek is an area known as Hell's Kitchen. This was the site of one of the early logging camps in the Gorge Area. The logging crews assembled here while they waited for the spring tides to float the logs downstream. The spot received its name because of the rugged terrain, the long wait, and the logging camp cooking.

LADY TIMMONS

On top of a lonely wind-swept point, in area of Swift Camp Creek, is the solitary grave of a woman who spent most of her life and considerable fortune pursuing a dream that failed to materialize—the search for the legendary lost silver mine described in the journal of John Swift.

She was "Lady" Rebecca P. Timmons. She and her husband had much wealth when they came to Wolfe County for recovering the lost silver lode. After several years of fruitless, searching Mr. Timmons health failed and they returned to New England. After her husband's death, she came back and continued the search. They had become extensive property owners, but one by one the properties were sold and the proceeds used for excavations for the fabled treasure. As her fortune dwindled, her workers became disheartened and pleaded with her to give up the search. She continued single-handedly until poverty and old age intervened.

She lived as a recluse in the Calaboose section of Wolfe County, her only companion be a small black and tan dog. Wherever she went, the dog would follow. The little faithful friend had not deserted her when the savings were gone. The dog preceded her in death. She supervised the burial and selected a spot along side for her own resting place.

The graves are located in the Calaboose section, within a few miles of the famous Rock Bridge. Not far away is an area still known as the "Timmons Diggins." Timmons Arch, named for this unusual lady, is on a high cliff overlooking Swift Camp Creek near its junction with Wildcat Branch.

Lady Timmons had lived in a small cabin at the foot of the knoll where she is buried. At that time, it was dense, sparsely settled, and scenic.

Recently, in the company of a local resident, I revisited her gravesite, after an absence of many years. Now houses are nearby and the grave was covered over with fallen timber. The final sojourn of a very unusual woman who brought color and excitement into the region should not be allowed to fade into obscure pages of history. An appropriate marker should be established to mark her interment and contribution to the history of the Red River Gorge.

The 1870 Wolfe County Census lists Rebecca P. Timmons as 43 years of age.

RED RIVER VALLEY RAILROAD

Around 1892 a narrow gauge (36") railroad was constructed from Rothwell to the top of the ridge south of Frenchburg. The steep grade was ascended by means of four switchbacks. The line proved to be a failure and was purchased by the Union City Lumber Company of Union City, Michigan. This company had

acquired large tracts of timber around Big Amos and Indian Creek. This was known as the Red River Tract and extended from Rt 460 in Menifee County to Powell County, containing over 6000 acres. The Red River Valley Railroad was incorporated May 19, 1898. The new construction ran to McCausey Ridge, which was named after the president of the RRVRR. This section was completed in 1898 and nine miles of the railroad was placed in operation. S.S. Pinney was named superintendent of the line. In 1899, a branch line was constructed which made a junction about two miles west of McCausey and was named Amos. The line continued in a southerly direction from Big Amos Creek to Apperson, named after Lewis Apperson, at the junction of East Fork of Indian Creek for an additional 5 miles.

Rolling stock of the Red River Valley Railroad included three climax locomotives, about 10 coal cars, 16 lumber flats and a

small combine. Locomotive No.1 was known as "Old Jim."
Another was Kitty Flyer.

Benton Dorset worked a brakeman for this railroad. He fell off
the train near McCausey Ridge and was run over by the train
crushing his leg. Dr Reese Kash amputated the leg above the
knee.

Dick Lyons was born in 1879. At eighteen, he married and set
up housekeeping in a cabin on Indian Creek. He established his
own sawmill and sawed for the Union City Lumber Company.

About 1889 the
timber off the Red
River Tract was
sold to Pryor,
Button and Garret.
This company hired
Harve and King
Tackett to do the
logging, which
continued until
1896. In this same
year the property
was sold by B.J.
Peters to J. Will Clay who hired Mort Powell and Tom Wells to
cut some of the timber. From the years 1896 to 1903, this land
was known as the Clay, Apperson and French. A. Nolan farmed
the land as a tenant until Lewis Apperson sold it to Bruce
Northcutt.

In 1904, the Big Woods Lumber Company bought timber off
this tract from Lewis Apperson. They built a railroad, set up a
large band mill near Powell Branch in an area now known as

Band Mill Bottom. They also set up a portable mill north of Band Mill, and logged several year.

Opal Smallwood was the last logger of the Indian Creek area. He logged Little East Fork of Indian Creek about 1964.

As long as the lumber business flourished, so did the Red River Valley Railroad. After the important timber stands had been removed, the railroad was scrapped during the latter part of 1911. The Three Climax locomotives were shipped to various points outside Kentucky.

In the year 1900, Shelby Palmer built a schoolhouse at the junction of Indian Creek and Big Amos. By the 1930's the school was discontinued and the old schoolhouse was now being used as a barn.

About 1900 Lester Jewell built a house near the junction of Big and Little Amos Creeks. The last occupant of the house was Garret Lawson, tenant of C.D. Williams who sold the property to the government in 1941.

A few loose foundation rocks are all that is left of the terminus of the Red River Valley Railroad at Apperson.

AN INCIPIENT INDUSTRY

Based on available information no large-scale niter mining operations are known to have occurred in the Red River Gorge. While evidence remains of hundreds of old "workings" in various states of preservation, these apparently were small group or individual efforts, which reached a numerical peak during the Civil War. The actual niter extraction process will not be examined here. Refer to "From Rockshelter to Gun barrel" for this method. Instead, we will focus on the different types of construction techniques used in the Red River Gorge.

Examination of the significant number of small niter mines within the rock shelters indicates three distinct types of hopper construction. Whether these were used in different times periods or as personal preference of the builder is unknown.

TYPE 1. Simply constructed of small poles supported by forked uprights. The resulting rough square was lined with heavy pieces of bark (usually hemlock) forming an apex as a "V" along the bottom just above a half-log trough.

TYPE 2 The hopper was constructed in the general form of a "V"by using a framework of bored logs to support the sloping sides of usually "rived" (hand-hewn, squared -up) boards. The

boards terminated nto a hollowed to half-log which acted as a gutter to carry off the liquid.

TYPE 3 Constructed of large hand-hewn single boards, which formed the sides and were held in place by a removable interlocking brace. The sides were only sloping slightly inward. Smaller boards placed upright on each end of the structure behind the cross-brace formed the ends. The entire structure was built over the collection trough, which was placed in position first. According to some "old timers", the entire system was portable and may have been dismantled and moved to other nearby locations. The would have eliminated the construction of new hoppers and troughs when one location was worked out and another started. This may explain the use and scarcity of this type construction.

The remains of Types 1 and 2 hoppers are relatively common in the Gorge. Type 3 is known to exist in only two places, giving substantial support to the theory these were portable and moved from location to location. One of these remains in good condition and is now enclosed, including the top, with a chain link fence so it might be preserved for future generations.

Niter mining played an important role in the settlement of America's frontier, the outcome of two wars, and involved some of our most notable figures in politics (Burr and Jefferson) and industry (Dupont). These Red River Gorge sites are significant and should be considered as an integral part of this areas historic heritage.

A BRIEF LOGGING HISTORY OF THE RED RIVER

The first record of logging activities in the Red River Gorge was in 1854 when Powell Rose cut timber in the Gladie Creek area. The original document is reproduced in its entirety below.

In 1886, the Kentucky Union Railroad Company established the Red River Lumber Company, and obtained deeds to nearly 4000 acres of land along the North Fork of Red River. Eight years later, the Red River Lumber Company was sold to Inman and Swan of New York, and the name changed accordingly. Under the leadership of these two men, this company prospered to become the second largest in the world and launched Clay City, Kentucky onto the map.

The company was sold again in 1900 to become the Clay City Lumber and Stave Mill. Floyd Day, who later established the Mountain Central Railroad, was the principal stockholder. In conjunction with James Swan, they purchased the company in 1902 as the Swann-Day Lumber Company. In 1904, Swann sold his interest to Floyd Day and the name was changed to Day Lumber and Coal Company. The same year Day sold to the Security Warehouse Company.

The Center Lumber Company was established in 1892. Six years later, it became the Climax Stave and Tie Company purchased by James B. Hall and J.H. Hardwick. C.H. Loveland and H.G. Garret bought the Tie and Stave Company in 1903. The Company changed hands again in 1905 becoming the Broadhead-Garret Lumber Company.

Dana Lumber Company of West Virginia purchased over 2500 acres in the Red River Gorge in 1909. This company was responsible for constructing the Nada Tunnel and a large band mill near the present day community of Nada. In fact, the community and tunnel were both named after the Dana Lumber Company, rearranging the syllables from Dana to Nada. Anagram of Dana.

Dana Lumber Company contracted with R.L. Sullivan to log the west side of Red River in 1913. The same year, the Sullivan Company cut and skidded 2,600,000 feet of timber off Fish Trap Branch alone.

In 1914, flames completely destroyed the Dana sawmill. Dana never rebuilt and transferred its entire acreage and appurtenances to the Broadhead-Garrett Company. This firm owned thousands of acres of timberland along Red River. They rebuilt the sawmill at Nada, and between 1914 and 1929 launched the most massive timbering effort in the history of the Red River. A system of "splash dams" was necessary to collect enough water to float logs headed for a boom near the mouth of Chimney Top Creek. The boom would catch the logs and hold them. In turn, a log loader would hoist the logs onto railroad cars for the journey to the mill at Nada.

Logs delivered to the mill from the Chimney Top and Dog Fork areas brought the following prices in 1907:

Poplar, cucumber, ash, white pine and walnut
$15.00/thousand feet
Hemlock and yellow pine   12.00   "
"
Chestnut, white oak, chestnut oak, maple   10.00   "
"

31

THE NADA TUNNEL

The Nada Tunnel is a large (13' x 12' x 900' long) bore constructed for the transportation of logs from the confines of the Red River Gorge by steam locomotives to the band sawmill at Nada on the L&E railroad. The Dana Lumber Company undertook this venture on November 22, 1910 by a contract with the firm of Swift and Weaver, railroad contractors from Charleston, West Virginia. The tunnel was to be constructed through the dividing ridge between Moreland Branch and Grays Branch. The contract stated the work would begin on or before the first day of December 1910 at $2.60 per cubic yard for the tunnel excavation and .45 cents per cubic yard for the approach.

On March 6, 1911, Swift (now Swift & Lacy) contracted with the firm of Fletcher and Snodgrass to begin work on the east end of the tunnel at $2.34 per cubic yard, moving not less than 24 cubic yards of material per day until they met with the excavating forces of the Dana Company working from the west end. Swift & Lacy failed to complete the contract after moving about 1757 cubic yards of material from the bore and Dana assumed the indenture on May 13, 1911 with an estimated 1900 cubic yards yet to remove. Swift & Lacy filed for bankruptcy on June 16, 1911.

Dana placed E.A. Simmons, who had been overseeing construction on the west end, in charge of both sides. At this time, Simmons was the vice president and general manager for Dana. Fletcher and Snodgrass (sub-contractors of Swift & Lacy) continued work on the east end, but were so far into the bore, the boiler would not supply sufficient steam to operate the drills. Simmons arranged for a large air compressor and boiler and positioned a pipeline across the divide from the west side to the east side providing air instead of the original steam power to operate the drills on both sides. On June 14, 1911, the Dana Lumber Company was reorganized with new officers.

D.S. McNitt   President
H. E. Shadle   Vice President
R. A. Harter   Secretary
W.O. Rearick   Treasurer and General Manager
A. Eckerson   Assistant Secretary

East and west end construction crews united on September 14, 1911, but it was not until early 1912 that the bore was passable for trains. The Dana firm continued laying the rail line on to Grays Branch, Fish trap, Tal Pal and Edwards Branch, transporting the logs to their band mill at Nada. One man and a dog were killed in an accidental explosion of dynamite in a storage area during the tunnel construction.

The band mill operated for two years and burned down in 1914. Dana sold to the Broadhead-Garret Lumber Company, who rebuilt the mill and continued operating the until 1920 when logging operations ceased, then sold the railroad, timber holdings and mill site. The mill was dismantled and moved to Tennessee. In 1934, Broadhead sold their holding to the U.S. Government for the establishment of the Cumberland National Forest.

During the period of the Broadhead-Garret operations, the company ran frequent excursions during the summer months from Nada to the Red River country. This service was rendered free of charge to church/picnic groups and for funerals.

According to old-timers, the railroad supported a 25 and 35-ton climax locomotives to haul the logs out of Red River. They recall the first load of logs through the tunnel created a log squeeze, compelling Dana to enlarge the bore to accommodate the sizeable logs that were typical of the area.

The Nada Tunnel is known today as the gateway to the Red River Gorge and is used by residents of the area and countless visitors. The number one photograph was taken in 1911 during construction on the east side and in the front row from left to right are Troy Spencer, James McCoy and Dock Spencer, forever cast as immortal in the chronicles of the Red River Gorge. The left photograph is a rockshelter on the east end of the tunnel used as a camp kitchen during the construction.

HIGH ROCK AND PINE RIDGE TOWERS

The High Rock Observatory was constructed in 1934 at a cost of $3000. The tower was 40 feet high with a 14 x14 foot wood cab. It was located in Powell County near the High Rock Settlement. The first resident was Kee Lewis, the last was Chester Morrison.

The Pine Ridge Lookout Tower was constructed in 1934 at a cost of $2000. The tower was 100 feet high with a 7x7 foot steel cab. It was located near the present day Koomer Ridge Campground. The tower was first occupied by Ollie Fanin and last by Leonard Brewer. Both towers were considered obsolete when the Forest Service chose aerial detection over the towers in the early 1970's. Both towers were sold by sealed bid shortly thereafter. Picture below is Pine Ridge and High Rock.

THE D. BOON HUT

More than any other man, Daniel Boone was responsible for the settlement of Kentucky. Boone's exploits as a backwoodsman and Indian fighter elevated him to folk hero status even during his early years. Boone had become a kind of patriarch not merely to Kentucky but to the entire nation as an individual who symbolized the frontier.

Perhaps one of the most controversial historic sites on the Red River is the D. Boon Hut. The crude structure, constructed of rived red oak boards is about 15 feet long, 10 feet wide and 4 feet high. The boards average about 3 feet in length and bear the marks of an ax. These are laid over a pole framework in an interlacing pattern with small stones holding them in place. Inside is a small open hearth while large sandstone boulders form the end walls. Nearby are two large stone rectangular fire hearths.

The hut is located inside a large rock shelter at the head of a deep cliff lined hollow in a rugged section of the Red River Gorge. The shelter measures about 230 feet in length with a maximum width of 114 feet. The ceiling rises approximately 35 feet above the floor at the mouth. Access to the shelter from the ridge top is limited.

The most thought-provoking aspects of the hut was one of shakes making up the roof bore the inscription "D. BooN" carved on the surface. The words were made by a series of holes in the pattern of letters.

37

The stipples were then connected by grooves to further form the letters. Note the absence of the "e" on Boone. It is a historical fact that Boone did not add the "e" to his name until after he came to Boonsboro in 1775. Since Carbon 14, dating is usually accurate to plus or minus 100 years, the error would be too great to be useful. Therefore, whether the carving is authentic may never be determined.

Other items discovered scattered about the floor of the shelter include a fragment of a shoe or moccasin, fragments of three ax hewn wooden troughs, two wooden paddles and pieces of an iron kettle. All of these are likely to be the remains of a niter mining operation either in the 1805-1814 period of during the War Between the States.

A most interesting aspect of the hut is the actual location. Constructed in a shallow hole, which appears to have been excavated by niter mining operations, the hut is well hidden from casual view. This significant fact indicates the hut may have been put together during the mining period or at least 36 years after Daniel Boone was supposed to have spent a winter in this area in 1769.

Other explanations include the hut was built by local boys in the 1920's from the remains of an old loggers cabin scattered about the floor of the rockshelter. Yet another, is the "D. BooN" board was carved by an individual, who is an avid muzzle-loader and frontiersman enthusiast who claims he carved Boone's name on a whim during one of his fall exploring excursions in the Gorge. Carving the name of famous idolized frontiersmen by such enthusiasts is quite similar to the thousands of Kilroy signatures, which appeared during World War II.

Another observation is that it is not likely, given the ever presence of hunting or war parties traveling the Warriors Path, that Boone would select a rockshelter at the head of a boxed in canyon offering little avenue for escape as his base camp.

None of these explains the board or shake with "D. Boon" carved on it. He may or may not have stayed in the area. However, the crude structure does reflect the culture of early settlers of the area and it should most certainty be preserved. A chain link fence in the front of the shelter is presently in place for this purpose.

The crude structure which was covered "with the dust of time" generated a deluge of newspaper articles, and gained national attention on April 2,1968 when the CBS Evening News ended its broadcast with Charles Kuralt at the site where Daniel Boone camped "in the days when the Kentucky Mountains were the Western Frontier", and commenting "Someday, no doubt, there will be a trail to this spot and vacationers, whole families, will come here to look through a fence at the cabin and stare at that legendary name caved on a board – "D. BooN". It is good, of course, that Americans have a sense of their history. We're glad we saw it this way, in the silence of the forest, under the great cathedral of protecting rock, the way it was left by whoever walked away from here 200 years ago".

Charles Kuralt, CBS, in the Red River Gorge, Kentucky; and, that's the way it is, Tuesday, April 2, 1968. This is Walter Cronkite, CBS News. Good night.

LOGGING TIGHT HOLLOW

On January 9, 1890 the Kentucky Union Land Company entered into a contract with S.M. Tutt to cut timber on Mill Creek in Powell and Wolfe Counties. Tutt had purchased the land from James Thomas and Bush & Ponder, lying on either side of Mill Creek or its tributaries to the top of the ridge, to a point one-fourth mile above the old mill site on Mill Creek and north of Brewer Grocery. Tutt was also to give Kentucky Union first refusal on timber in the upper part of Mill Creek. In addition, he was to put in Splash Dams plus clean up Mill Creek to facilitate logging, and build roads as well as houses.

For all this work, Tutt was to receive $5.00 per 1,000 ft. ($4.00 per 1,000 ft for bankside deliver and $1.00 per 1,000 ft for delivery at the mouth of Mill Creek).
Under the contract, Kentucky Union could stop the timber harvest and then pay damages to Tutt for stopping the work.

In addition, under verbal contract, Tutt could also cut and deliver to KU timber from land other than his. For this additional timber, Tutt would receive a total of $6.50 per 1,000 ft ($5.50 for bankside and $1.00 per 1,000 ft for delivery to the mouth of Mill Creek).

Under this contract, Tutt delivered on the bank 3,100, 000 ft of logs from his lands and delivered 400,000 ft of logs off other land. All were measured and marked KU by Kentucky Union.

Tutt also put up four Splash Dams on Mill Creek cleaned out rocks and obstructions and built roads and houses. He delivered 875,000 ft to the mouth of Mill Creek.

On January 9, 1891, Kentucky Union stopped Tutt from logging due to the "present or existing circumstances and unsettled conditions of the markets generally."

Tutt sued Kentucky Union claiming a lien on all logs, with the logs to go into receivership, and a judgment of $10,840 against Kentucky Union. In the court case, it was brought out that Kentucky Union was selling its assets in several counties, including Powell, Wolfe and Menifee. They had to file bankruptcy due to legal problems resulting from not acquiring all timber rights in the area.

In the 1930's and 1940's, Roscoe Meadows also logged in Tight Hollow, a branch of Mill Creek. The logs were hauled out of the prong over the cliff.

The Forest Service acquired the property in October 1934 from Ms. Golden Day for the establishment of the Cumberland National Forest (now Daniel Boone)

THE LEGEND OF STEVE DEHART

A cemetery at Nada, Kentucky contains a limestone slab, which marks the final resting place of a man who has become a local legend in Kentucky folklore. Bear hunter, explorer, rock climber, master storyteller, Steve Dehart has achieved a certain measure of immortality as long as the name Dehart Arches endure. Thomas Dehart journeyed from Bedford County, Virginia to Kentucky and migrated to Powell County sometime after 1839. He settled near the head of a hollow just east of the present day settlement of Nada, where Steve Dehart entered into the world on June 23, 1860. At an early age, Steve became interested in hunting and trapping and often accompanied his father on hunting trips into the Red River Gorge.

Steve Dehart was one of the most noted and colorful individuals to ever stride the cliff-studded valleys and rims of the Red River Gorge. Many legends and stories are centered about him. It is said he played a role in the establishment of Natural Bridge State Park in 1926. He is credited with climbing Pyramid Rock and leaving two gold coins on the summit of this prominence for anyone who could climb the rock. He made numerous trips to Ohio displaying his famed collection of Indian artifacts. Before his death in 1940, he supposedly selected his coffin, lined it with the bearskin killed on his last hunt, and lay down in the coffin to try it for fit! Such was the Steve Dehart legend.

In October 1901 on a high ridge overlooking Edwards Branch, Steve Dehart and his dogs cornered a bear along the edge of a high cliff. Sizing the animal, he realized it was the largest bear he had ever seen. It required eleven shots at close range to kill the enraged beast.

As the echo of that last shot rebounded through the rugged cliffs, it signified the passing of an era. Although Steve Dehart did not realize it at the time, he had killed the last wild bear in the Red River Gorge.

THE DEVIL WOMAN OF RED RIVER

Many years ago near Pinch-Um-Tight Gap in the Red River Gorge, there once lived an old woman and her family. According to stories handed down, she was supposed to have been very mean and was widely known for her "tincture of light foot". She was infamously dubbed "Devil Sal" or the "Devil Woman of Red River."

In those days, the entire family pitched in to help with the food supply. One fine late summer day, Devil Sal and her two sons set out for the top of a cliff where blueberries grew in profusion. The route to the rim was a long narrow crack in the face of the cliff. The children scrambled up easily, but Devil Sal being a somewhat robust woman, found the crack a tight fit. By maneuvering around and using small niches for hand and footholds, she finally managed to gain the top.

The view from this spiny prominence was superb; but Devil Sal's mind was not on the view. She had brought along two large tin buckets and her immediate concern was filling these with the berries. The bushes grew close together and the buckets were soon filled with the blue fruit.

When the family started down the crack in the cliff to the valley below, Devil Sal let, her children go first and they were soon down safely. Then she started to descend, and as she was carefully making her way, she became wedged in a tight spot. She placed the tin buckets on her shoulders in an effort to squirm free, but soon found herself in a position where she could go neither up nor down. Her children, seeing her quandary, ran off and left her tightly jammed in the crack.

After staying in this position for a period, she managed to free herself. There was considerable activity when she finally reached home.

That is why the cliff was named Pinch-Um-Tight Gap, the same name it bears today. It stands like a giant cenotaph to the memory of Devil Sal or the Devil Woman of Red River.

BREWER'S SHUTE

Jim Brewer studied the inimitable spiny prominences of the Red River Gorge from a high cliff near Osborne Ridge. However, his thoughts were not on this exceptional sculpture of nature's creation, but how best to remove the huge timber, which abounded in natural profusion on the ridge tops and valley's. Jim Brewer was an independent logger in the boom years of timbering and getting these fine specimens of trees to the market was his chief concern now.

Brewer faced a transportation problem: Moving the logs over the high cliffs to where they could expediently be moved to market. After considerable study, he decided to build a wooden "shute" (chute) through a gap in the cliff just below the roundabout to flume the logs from ridge top to valley. Undertaking the construction of this log flume was a somewhat larger job than he had anticipated, but eventually it was completed.

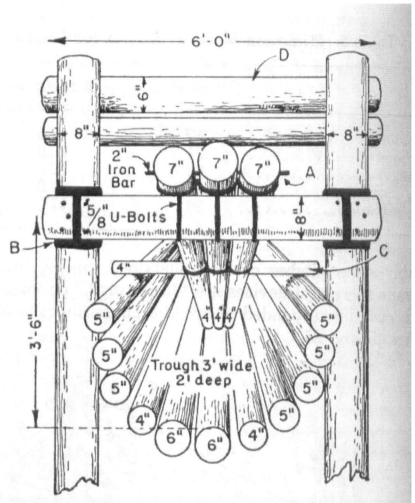

The "shute" was constructed of White Oak timber and stretched from the top of Osborne Ridge to a bench near Red River. A system of logs called Wolfe brakes was chained to the chute in such a manner (one or more logs with one end above the shute and the other end lying in the chute) to act as brakes to slow down the descent of the logs, as they were flumed to the valley. As the logs travel downward, they strike the Wolfe brake, which is knocked upward as the log passes through slowing the speed. According to some loggers, the speed was still fast enough to cause logs to fly out of the chute. The number of brakes needed was dependent upon the slope of the chute.

Brewer's Shute operated for a time, and then fell into disuse as logging operations was completed in the area. No trace of the Shute remains except for a short length of wire cable at the top. The area is still known as Brewer's Shute and is a local landmark.

THE CRANE TABLE

On the upper Red River in an area near the Roundabout is located an unobtrusive flat white rock of considerable magnitude. This rock was well known in older times and was called the Crane Table. During the late 1800's cranes were very numerous in the Red River Gorge. Old timers observed vast numbers of them flying overhead during migration periods for hours at a time raising an almost deafening clamor. Oftentimes the cranes would land conspicuously on this flat rock for short rest periods. Consequently, this rock became known as the Crane Table and is a local landmark.

THE ROUNDABOUT

The Roundabout is a long-forgotten name along the upper Red River. According to some old-timers, the roundabout is a very tight bend just below Clifty Creek. During the famous "June Tide" of June 26, 1882, the river almost completely swirled around the bend a second time. Hence the name Roundabout. I have visited this area and due to the high cliff-lined channel it would appear this could happen given the sufficient amount of volume that must have existed during the "June Tide" which it is said the like has never been seen before or since. The tide occurred before the blowing of "Old 96" which is in the same general location.

CHRONICLE ON THE ROCK

From Laurel Fork in the Red River Gorge comes a tale as strange as it is sorrowful. The story relates an event that must have stamped a strong impression on the carvers mind. It was told this way to me.

In a remote drainage of Laurel Fork, there lived an old settler and his two stalwart sons whose intense pride was their horses. In due, time the old man passed on. His sons decided to take him to a cemetery some distance away for his last piece of earth. After making the coffin, the sons placed it on a wagon hitched to their prized horses, and started the old man's final sojourn. The route out led over a steep cliff barely negotiable by wagon and team. The sons began to argue over which horse could pull the most loads. During the course of this verbal disagreement, as they were on the steep cliff, the coffin somehow slipped from the wagon and pounded over the rim rock. One son became so angry at this turn of events; he shot and killed his brother. In the days that followed, while waiting for the law, his remorse became so great he was moved to carve the story in stone at the cliff edge. The events are depicted in rock by these symbols:

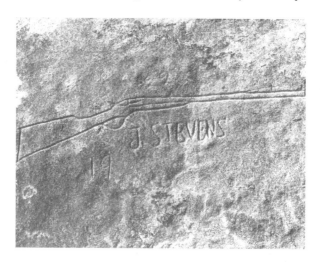

The J Stevens represents the weapon used, along with the .38 revolver. The watch tells the time of day and the hand represents the arm of the law. The date is obscure, but this happened in the 1930's. Several more carvings are located on this rock.

50

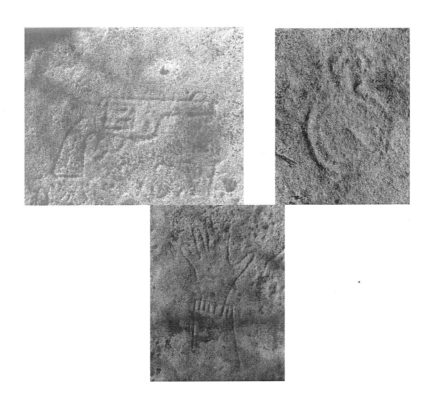

MOUNTAIN CENTRAL RAILROAD

 The Mountain Central Railroad was built by Floyd Day in 1898. The purpose was to carry timber from his lumber camps in sections of Powell and Wolfe Counties to the Swan-Day Lumber Mill at Clay City. The 12-mile narrow gauge line (36") climbed the ridge of the Junction by a series of switchbacks, and then descended Chimney Top Creek to Red River.

As the Red River forest was worked out, a new line was built along Pine Ridge to Campton. The rails reached Pine Ridge in the spring of 1906. In the fall of 1907, the little Climax locomotives entered Campton and the entire line was placed in operation

When the logging operations were finished, the line was to be abandoned, but the people of Wolfe County asked Floyd Day to extend the line to Campton Junction for a passenger line and freight train. Mr. Day agreed to this proposal and the line remained in operation until 1928 for this purpose. The rails were left intact until 1930 when dismantling of the line started.

This was a narrow gauge line and when the train labored up some of the steepest grades, old timers who had ridden the tracks, said that one could get off behind the train and walk, keeping pace with the train. This was especially true if the train was heavily loaded.

Due to numerous cliffs along the route, the MCR line abounded in trestles and hairpin turns. The course was very scenic, ascending the slopes by means of switchbacks following the ridges through Chimney Top, Pine Ridge, High Falls and Duff siding to Campton. If this line were in operation today, it would surely be one of the largest tourist attractions in the entire region.

THE CRASH OF A DINKY

The little Mountain Central Railroad, built in 1898, enjoyed an impeccable safety record until that fateful Saturday evening of October 21, 1904. Around 5:30 pm, the engineer, Bud Smith, had trouble in controlling the engine as he proceeded down a steep grade into Whittleton Branch.

As the train with four cars descended the grade, the speed increased and all hands were put to work at the brakes, which were set and reset, in the hope the speed could be checked. All efforts were in vain. The train actually increased in speed on the steep grade despite the brakes. The conductor, Charles Lythe, realizing the cars would jump the tracks if the speed were not reduced, crawled out on the cowcatcher of the reversed engine and sprinkled sand on the track. William McNabb, a brakeman, followed the example of Lythe and assisted him in sprinkling the sand on the track.

Thee train had traveled about a half mile from the crest of the grade when it crashed into a cliff extending from the side of the tracks.

Lythe and Smith were caught beneath the engine, which was turned on its side.
Death was instantaneous to both. Joseph Derickson, a sawmill engineer, was on a car loaded with cross ties and was caught under them, the ties crushing his legs to his body. He was very cool and bore his suffering bravely, giving advice to his

rescuers as too how to quickest move the great mass of wreckage piled on him.

He told his companions. "He was suffering at present, but would soon rest." After shaking hands with many of those present and telling them "good-bye, he gave up the ghost at 10:00pm. It is a remarkable fact the line had been in operation for six years, often handling nine cars on this grade without an accident.

LAST SETTLER ON ROCK BRIDGE

The Rock Bridge Nature Trail meanders through scenic stands of White Pine and Rhododendron thickets eventually crossing a small knoll through a long since abandoned field. It is on this knoll that a few loose rocks mark the old dwelling of the last settler on Rock Bridge.

Sam Duff was an employee of the Broadhead and Garrett Lumber Company. He operated the splash dams in Swift Creek and below Rock Bridge. In his spare time, he farmed the area around his residence.

The Duff's crossed Swift Creek on the now famous Rock Bridge and continued out Red Hill to Campton for their trips into town. A school was located at Quillen Chapel and involved a three-mile walk for the children.

Around 1906, Sam Duff moved to the top of the ridge in order to live on a good road. He released the last logs through the splash dams in 1910, thus bringing to a close a brief and vibrant period in the history of the Red River Gorge.

TRAGEDY AT NADA TUNNEL

The day was windy and temperatures were well below zero. This was typical weather for a February day of 1911. Work was progressing well on the railroad tunnel and hopes were high that it would be completed by the year's end. On this particular day, February 12th, blasting operations were scheduled. Charles McNabb, a 19 year old, was assigned he task of retrieving dynamite from the storage area. A hard freeze had gripped the area for the past few days and when Charles removed the explosives, they were frozen solid. He took the dynamite to a large rockshelter where he kindled a fire in order to facilitate thawing. Having used this procedure before, he gave little thought to the hazards of such an undertaking. Instead, he arranged the dynamite around the fire in such a manner that thawing would be possible.

While waiting for the explosives to thaw, Charles let his mind wander ahead to when the time the tunnel would be completed and logging operations would begin. Maybe he could engineer one of the trains. Yes, he would soon be through with the tunnel.

As he sat engrossed in his thoughts, the unattended fire became larger and flames began to creep towards the explosives. The flames moved stealthily nearer and nearer until there was a tremendous explosion and Charles was through with the tunnel...Forever!

Circumstances surrounding the explosion were vague; however, it is possible the fire set off a hidden cap, thus initiating the detonation. Another young man by the name of Townsend was injured and a dog was killed.

The rockshelter is visible from KY 77 near the east end of the tunnel and untold numbers of visitors pass by unaware of the tragedy of 1911.

OLD 96

On a lonely rugged stretch of the upper Red River Gorge, a huge boulder stands in mute testimony to the bygone years of the logging industry during the latter part of the 18th century. Known locally as "Old 96" this mass of rock once reached nearly across the width of the river, effectively channeling the stream flow through a narrow opening.

As timbering began in the upper gorge, the logs were floated downstream and logjams were common at Old 96. After a brief period of these jams, it was decided to blow apart the boulder to allow free passage. Thinking it would be a simple task, the supervisor sent one of the powdermen to attend to the job early one morning. When the man failed to return by late evening, the supervisor became concerned and set out to search for him. About the same time the powdermen, tired, wet and hungry showed up at the logging camp. When questioned why it had taken so long to blow the boulder apart, he replied it had taken 96 kegs of powder to blow the passage. From that day forward, the rock was known as "Old 96".

The remains of the boulder are located about halfway between the Swift Creek Bridge and Clifty Creek, with drill marks still clearly visible over its scarred surface.

ROCK BRIDGE GRIST AND CARDING MILL

In the years before the War Between the States, mountain folks on foot or horseback frequented the rugged domain of Swift Creek taking their tuck of wool or measure of grain to Drake's Mill on Rock Bridge Fork.

During the years of the mid -1800's James Drake discovered near the junction of Swift Creek and Rock Bridge Fork, what seemed to be an ideal location for a water mill at a falls. He built a dam and a house for the burrstone to grind corn and wheat. He also installed a machine for carding wool. An 1870 Manufactures census, PRODUCTS OF INDUSTRY lists the following for the carding machine and grist mill in Precinct No.3, Wolfe County, Kentucky, during the year ending June 1, 1870, as enumerated by James C. Holder, Ass't Marshal.

NAME OF BUSINESS: ROLLS
Name of Company: DRAKE, JAMES
Capital Invested: $2000
Hands employed per year: 1 male over 16 years & 1 female above 15 years
Number of months in active operation: 5

POWER USED IN MANUFACTURING: WATER
Machines: Name or description -Carding
Machines: Number of - 2
Horsepower: 4

MATERIALS
Wool: 8,450 lbs
Value: $3,380

PRODUCTS

Rolls: 8,400 lbs
Value: $4,000

FLOUR & MEAL

Name of business: DRAKE, JAMES
Capital invested: $150
Hands employed per year: 1male over 16 years
Number of months in active operation: 12
Estimated maximum daily capacity in bushels: 50
Percent of grinding performed for custom or market: All custom

POWER USED IN MANUFACTURING: Water
Machines: Name or description - Grinding
Machines: Number of -two
Horsepower: four

MATERIALS
Wheat: Number of bushels- 200
Value: $200
Corn: Number of bushels -2,400
Value: $1,200

PRODUCTS
Flour: 40 barrels
Value: $400
Meal: 2700 bushel
Value: $1,350

The 1880 Manufacturers Census PRODUCTS OF INDUSTRY in the 4th precinct, Wolfe County, Kentucky, beginning June 1, 1879, and ending May 31, 1880, enumerated by I. W. Mapel. Supervisor's Dist. No. 5. Enumeration Dist. No.118. This census lists the business as John E. Drake rather than James, and in the fourth precinct instead of the third. This may be the mill listed on Swift Creek about one mile downstream from Rock Bridge Fork. Two mills are noted on an 1875 map.

FLOURING AND GRIST MILLS
Name of business: Drake, John E.
Capital invested $400
Hands employed per year: two (2 male over 16 with line drawn through 1)
Number of hours per day labor: May to November - 10
    "   " "   "   "   "   : November to May - 8
Day's wages of skilled mechanic: $1.00
Day's wages of ordinary laborer: .50
Total annual wages paid $75
Months in operation per annum: 7
Months idle: five
Number of runs of Stones: one
Estimated maximum daily capacity in bushels: 75
Percent of grinding performed for custom or market: all custom

POWER USED IN MANUFACTURING: WATER
Name of stream: Swift Creek –Red River
Height of fall in feet: 12
Number of wheels: one
Kind of wheel: Reaction
Breadth in feet: 2 1/2
Revolutions per minute: 250
Horsepower: 10?

MATERIALS
Number of bushels of wheat: 200
Value: $200
Number of bushels of other grain: 1,500
Value: $950
Value of mill supplies: $50
Total value of all materials: $1,200

PRODUCTS
Number of barrels of wheat flour: 40
Number of pounds of corn meal: 75,000
Number of pounds of feed: 9,000
Value of all other products: not listed
Total value of all products: $1,400

A trip to the mill was a long, rough journey via the old state
road below Hazel Green, then to Clarks Ford of Red River, Up
Clarks Branch and into the breaks of Stillwater Creek, finally
crossing Tutt's Ford, a swift and difficult crossing. The traveler
then scaled the cliffs to Little Calaboose Ridge and faced a
difficult trip descending down through the gaps and benches of
Swift Camp Creek where he crossed the famous Rock Bridge
and reached the end of his journey. Because of the location of
the mill and the long, rough trip, it eventually fell into disuse.

The mill later washed out in what is known as the "June Tide"
of June 26, 1882. George Hardman using steam power rebuilt

the mill. The mill operated until 1910 when it exploded, killing Hardman and destroying the mill.

A few notches cut into the rock above the falls are all that remains and these, in time, will erode away obliterating the last vestige of Drakes Mill.

THE GLADIE CREEK HISTORIC SITE

One of the early settlements in the Red River Gorge was at Gladie Creek, a tributary of Red River that flows northwest through Menifee County. The old log cabin on the site was built sometime during this settlement. The cabin was recently restored in 1988, and is currently being used as an interpretive center emphasizing the logging industry in the Gorge between 1880-1920.

According to records, the first individual to ever own land at Gladie was a person by the name of Dean Timmons. He was apparently a revolutionary war soldier and was given a land grant of 22,000 acres in 1786 by the Commonwealth of Virginia. There is no evidence that Timmons ever resided, or even visited, Gladie, and by the 1870's the land appears to have been considered unclaimed.

 In 1873, records indicate that James Spencer owned 500 acres at the mouth of Gladie Creek. In the same year, Spencer sold that tract to Franklin Ballenger Ledford. Franklin sold the land in 1880 to Noble Ledford for $725. The land was then passed to James Ledford in 1882. Although somewhat unclear, James Ledford appears to have passed to land to his nephew, Joseph B. Ledford. Joseph later owned most of the property on Chimney Top Creek and Wolf pen Creek as well.

 In 1937, Joseph Ledford deeded the last of his property on Gladie to his daughter Nellie Ledford Gibbs, who had married Stanley Gibbs and lived in the old house at Gladie. In fact, it was Stanley around 1914 who built the frame house around the old cabin. While building

the chimney, a stone was inscribed with "Billie" and placed on the stonework of the chimney. Billie was the son of Stanley and Nellie Gibbs. The stone is still visible today. The property changed hands several times in the intervening years before finally being secured in Government ownership in 1987.

 Subsistence farming was a means to earn a living. The soil was rich and produced good crops of tobacco, corn and sorghum cane. On occasions, the crops would be flooded out by the Red River, which caused economic disaster and hardship for the families. If the food crops were destroyed, the family looked to the woods to provide meat, nuts, and berries and paw paws. Hunting was not limited to the men folks. Stella Tackett, mother of the famous Lily Mae Ledford was a hunter within her own right. She was the wife of White Ledford.

 Powell Rose logged documents show Gladie as early as 1854. The subsequent years brought a massive onslaught of logging to this area. Getting the timber out of this rugged area was a real task. Horses, mules or oxen were used to pull the logs down to the creeks. Splash dams were built across the creeks to impound the water to build up a pool. When the spring rains came, the logs were rolled into the streams and the dams were triggered to release the gate and a torrent of water along with a loud splash. The logs were carried on this surge to the next dam where the process was repeated. Sometimes, logjams occurred. An old-timer tells about one at the mouth of Gladie Creek (Gladie had seven dams) that was a mile long and contained an estimated thirty-five to fifty thousand logs. The logs had to be blasted free in this particular jam, but crews could usually find a key log that was holding the jam and by releasing it, free the rest of the logs.

Several families lived up and down Gladie Creek in Sargent, Klaber, and Hale Branches. It is known that a house was a Klaber Branch in 1894. The White Ledford family lived there for a time in the 1920's and moved to Chimney Top Creek after been flooded out. This was Lily Mae Ledford's family. She and her sisters, Rosie and Susie, were the famous Coon Creek Girls. They were America's first all girl string band which played regularly at Renfro Valley.

The center for this little community was at the mouth of Gladie, near the cabin site. There was a school, a post office and a cemetery. Many residents traveled to Pomeroyton where there was doctor, church and stores. There was a small store at Gladie operated by Bill Profit. No record exists of a church building in the area, although one of the dwellings may have been used.

This 1926 picture of the Gladie School reveals a one-room school. It was probably built about 1906. Some of the Ledford's taught there at one time or another. Some years the school was only open for three months of the year because the boys had to work. The school was closed in 1926 causing the local children to attend school at Big Woods on Tarr Ridge. The school building was torn down sometime in the early 1930's and the boards used to build the house at Pumpkin Bottom.

A U.S. Post Office was established at Gladie on June 11, 1884 with the following postmasters of record:

June 11, 1884	Benjamin H. Noe
May 14, 1886	Alley Ledford
Nov 17, 1886	Will Ledford
April 23, 1887	Post Office discontinued, moved to Mariba.

The Post Office was reestablished on August 30, 1900, apparently to serve the massive logging operations in progress at this time;

August 30, 1900   Isaac N. Horton
January 18, 1902   Julia F. Klaber
May   02 1905   Joseph B. Ledford
Nov   21, 1905   Closed, moved six miles downstream to
Haystack.

 Stanley and Nellie occupied the house from about 1918-1953. They added the siding and additional rooms. The house was complete. It had water piped from a spring under a cliff. Natural gas was piped from a well located near the present location of the sorghum mill. Arch Carpenter drilled this well in 1937. The gas was used for lights, refrigerator and a heating system. Besides the cabin, there was a chicken house, two barns, a smokehouse and corncrib.

Today, thousands of visitors come to this site. Like you, they learn about the early days and the people who first ventured into this wild country to live and raise their families. It is easy to imagine how they could have been drawn to the rugged beauty of this area.

THE SWIFT CAMP CREEK DELUGE

The morning of July 5, 1939 dawned dark and ill-omened with massive thunderheads banking in the east as Henry Swango arranged his day. Henry lived on a small farm at the confluence of Swift Camp Creek and Red River and this appeared to be just another day of toil. Little did Henry know that before this day was out, his entire farm would be destroyed by water and he was fortunate not to have lost his life in the deluge! However, this was still hours in the future. Henry's immediate concern was tending his crops and the myriad other chores a farmer must do. Suddenly, stillness fell upon the land and a chill was in the air. Henry looked up from work and gazed around, somewhat ill at ease. Something seemed amiss. Without any more warning, a tidal wave of water rocketed down Swift Camp Creek, sweeping away his house, barn and all the crops into Red River. This occurred from cloudbursts near the headwaters of Swift Creek and in neighboring Breathitt County where a reported twenty-foot wall of water came roaring down the Frozen Creek Valley causing many deaths, with destruction written in terms of hundreds of thousands of dollars. After viewing the devastation to his farm, Henry decided to settle elsewhere, and did not rebuild.

Pictured below is the farm on Swift Creek, before the Frozen Creek flood when the first bridge across Red River was being constructed.

A GATHERING AT GLADIE CREEK

The Gladie Creek Historic Site began as a conceptual image. In the early 1960's the old cabin was shrouded in pine siding and was being used to store hay. After receiving permission from the landowner, some of the inside boards were removed exposing the poplar logs and dovetail notches. This revelation began a vision of restoration that has spanned well over a quarter century. In this long neglected historical relic, unlimited possibilities for interpreting the history of the area unfolded.

Throughout the years, several efforts by the U.S. Forest Service to purchase the property were futile. It was not until 1987, through the efforts of the Nature Conservancy, the property was finally secured in federal ownership. The long heralded vision of restoration begins to achieve a measure of reality.

Restoration of the site began in 1988, after basic stabilization of the cabin. This was a tremendous undertaking and there was much speculation on how best to start. It was decided to offer the visitors and communities an opportunity to physically participate in the restoration of the site by participating in old-fashioned "Workings." In days of yore, joint work parties, uniting for the common good, could accomplish so much more than an individual or family working alone. Cabins and barns that could take a man alone weeks or months to build were often erected in a single day by a "working." These "workings" also gave people an opportunity to socialize, let off seam and catch up on visiting and conversation.

71

With this spirit of cooperation in mind, several such old-fashioned "workings" were held at Gladie with extraordinary results. Such things as splitting shingles for the cabin roof, removing the old roof, placing new shingles, fireplace, flooring, to name a few.

The response to these "workings" was little short of miraculous, involving resident and officials of five counties and visitors from as far away as California. Three hundred and fifty volunteers expended over eight thousand person-hours to insure the success of this project while at the same time making a priceless investment in the past.

During this time, several interpretive events were scheduled such as a homecoming, sorghum making from cane grown on the site, story telling, old time crafts, and many others. Later, Living Archaeology weekend was added along with things such as a tribute to Lily Mae Ledford, log brands, an old-fashioned Christmas at Gladie, and old-time quilts, all centered around the cabin.

One of the Gladie highlights was a visit from a 32 member choral group from the Soviet Union. They were treated to a traditional Kentucky dinner and afterwards invited to

participate in the sorghum making in progress at that time
They responded by singing several Russian Folk Songs in
acappella chorus. Towards the end of the last number, a
wonderful thing happened. In a spontaneous gesture of
friendship, Russians and Kentuckians joined hands in an
impromptu polka around the field.

The restoration of this historic site combined with the on-going
interpretive programs has attracted thousands of visitors. These
visitors are gaining a new understanding of the history of the
area along with an appreciation for the wise use of natural and
cultural resources.

This unique opportunity
would not have been possible
without the dedicated efforts
of so many. The restoration
program was led by the U.S.
Forest Service but was
supported by local
communities adjacent to the
cabin. The project has
instilled a sense of pride and
ownership in the people of a
five county area. This old
cabin, once thought to be

imperiled by vandalism, is now literally protected by these same
people.

The project improved Kentucky's cultural resources by
involving the public in a number of projects that clearly
represent the manner in which our ancestors lived.
The restoration of the log structure has provided an educational
tool to unite the past and present for the coming generations by
focusing on the role of natural resources in the settlement of

73

Gladie Creek, Menifee County, the State of Kentucky, and indeed, the entire nation.

This activity has provided three wonderful things:
Provided security for an isolated historic site.
Given local residents an increased pride in their heritage.
Provided a use for the land that has the potential to benefit millions of people.

"UNCLE" BILLY BOWEN

The community of Bowen, Kentucky is located about three miles east of the county seat of Stanton. Quiet now, with little relations to the days when it was an important stop on the L & N Railroad. Bowen was where "Uncle" Billy called home. He was reputed to be the strongest man in the county, easily lifting barrels of bolts no other man could budge.

A store was the gathering place for Bowen residents. Two stores were on opposite sides of the road, one the general store, being on the side of the hill and frequented by the ordinary folks, and the other often referred to as the "Den of Sin" where the liquid (not water) flowed freely. The store was owned and operated by Billy Townsend. A widow woman lived nearby with two grown sons who were regular visitors at the Den of Sin. This caused the widow much exasperation and as the days faded into months, it became increasingly worse.

One day the widow was in the general store where she encountered Uncle Billy and poured out her tale of woe, finishing with the fact her sons were over there at this very moment, and how she wished the place would burn down. Uncle Billy, being a devilish sort of fellow, replied, "Why not blow it up with a stick of dynamite."

A few days later, the widow sought out Billy and told him she had all she could take; she just could not take anymore, and requested the dynamite he had mentioned before. Billy told her he would have it for her the next day. After some thought Uncle Billy obtained a mailing tube, painted it red and packed it with mud; inserting a real fuse so it resembled an actual stick of dynamite. This he gave to the widow the next day instructing her on how to light the fuse.

Taking the stick of "dynamite" in hand the widow marched over to the den, threw open the door and announced her intentions of blowing the place to hell. Being winter, there was a fire in the pot-belled stove in the center of the room. The widow struck the match, lit the fuse and tossed the "dynamite" into the room. It was immediately grabbed by one of the patrons and flung back toward the door. It struck the wall and bounced back into the room coming to rest under the stove! There was a wild rush toward the back door. In the stampede, the stove was knocked over and the den was aflame.

Uncle Billy, at the general store, was bent double with laughter.

ELIJAH SARGENT

Elijah Sargent was something of a legend on Parched Corn Creek. There are tales of him killing a panther with an axe and eating rattlesnake hearts to make him brave. At the time of his death on September 1, 1932, he resided in a small log house near the mouth of Parched Corn Creek. He was 61 years old. It is rumored he died from gangrene beginning from an unattended gun shot wound.

Elijah and family moved to Parched Corn Creek sometime around 1910, (five sons, and one daughter) while W.A. Clark, Matt Clay and others were cutting the timber. He lived in a small house, which was built for logging purposes. In 1914 when this house burned, Elijah and his family moved on the opposite side of Parched Corn to a small logging shanty for about 8 months while he constructed the log cabin at the mouth of the creek. In 1924, Elijah's wife Fannie together with their three sons still at home moved away from the property to Dog Creek, leaving Elijah on Parched Corn. One of the sons, Abraham, returned a short time later and lived with his father until his death in 1932 Hobart and Mitchell would go back on occasion to help their father farm, planting and tending corn and oats in the cleared areas. Little is known about Butler, who left the creek in about 1917. Elhannan Sargent enlisted in the army in 1918 and was killed in action the same year. Mae left the creek about 1917. In 1934, Abraham still resided on Parched Corn Creek.

IT IS WRITTEN – ON STONE

It has been many years since I observed my first petroglyph and reflected upon the strange rock art. This was my introductory alliance with these carvings on stone, which has spanned over 40 years. During the spread of these years, it was my uncommon privilege to discover nearly 100 such symbols where ancient man shaped his message. This includes the unprecedented finding of the Trinity Rock Shelters and the most unique rock art in the Red River Gorge, if not the entire nation. Sadly, in recent years, a thoughtless or uncaring camper built his fire squarely on this ancient manuscript, destroying irretrievable the long carved message.

Observe this carving closely. Just above the scale is an inverted "V" known as a vulvaform design and represents the female. Immediately above this is a so called "stick man" that symbolizes the male. About mid center to the right is an outline of a child's foot. Man, woman and child symbols probably depicting the birthplace of an important figure. Note the series of small "v" across the top of the rock. This significant record in stone has vanished forever.

The Red River Gorge is a land of edges, steep valleys and high sheer cliffs. Geologic erosion has worn away the softer rock forming a definite cliff line abounding with rock shelters, natural arches and rock outcrops. Most of the rock shelters show convincing evidence of human occupation. In many of the shelters a section of overhanging cliff has fallen forward providing a convenient working ledge at the shelter entrance. On some of these working ledges are found petroglyphs.

Petroglyph is a word of Greek origin from petro (rock) and glyph (carving). The word is defined as a carving or an inscription on a rock. The carvings are usually cut to a depth of ¼ to 1 inch with smoothing out by abrading. They are completely incised, not jut outlined, leaving little doubt as to what the author intended to depict.

The ancients recorded their history through these scribings on rock, and retelling of legends. Major events that were important to them appear in some petroglyphs. There are those who believe these primeval writings are mere doodling, and if they had any meaning at all, it perished with the individual who carved them. Conversely, in the Red River Gorge, the similarity of tracks, circles and other symbols far removed from each other suggests these carvings were much more than an aimless scribble to help pass the long winter months in the rock shelters.

This picture writing is a modern day cryptogram. Was the intent of the original author art or communication? There appears to be a great deal of evidence to support the rationale that most of the carved symbols are common to rock writing and therefore a defined linguistic attribute. If artistic expression had been the original intent of the writers, it seems reasonable they would have selected smooth writing surfaces. Many such smooth rock faces were often ignored in favor of uneven ones in the petroglyphs of the Red River Gorge. However it is impossible to know the exact intention of the original author. An interesting example is the human footprints. Note the four toes common to carvings of this type in the Red River Gorge.

It has been many years since the valleys rang to the sharp sound of flint on stone as the ancient artist shaped his message, and the now forgotten trails felt the tread of his moccasined feet. Likewise, all early humankind has disappeared along with the true meaning of the time when man first expressed his reasoning on the sandstone boulders.

There is an intriguing possibility the nation's petroglyphs had a common origin with some Old World petroglyphs at some place on the other side of the globe, or at least were influenced by them.   This ancient scribing of early man's inscriptions is perhaps the earliest form of a written language.

A passage in Genesis 11, 1 is a reminder: "And the whole earth was of one language and one speech." Petroglyphs are to be found in every quarter of the earth with vast similarity. Perhaps this may serve as a testimony that a written language was understood over the entire world.

The inscribed faces of Red River Gorge rocks and their kindred over the earth have endured the tortures of millenniums, silent in forbearance, waiting for humankind to decipher the message and in gratitude travel onward/upward toward their destiny.

And what a cause for gratitude! Man may have learned of how and when these inscriptions came to be distributed "all over the earth" by "people of one language."

Such knits well with Holy writ (Genesis 11: 1-9), and in the presence of such truth, in my humble insignificance, I can only testify: "It is written – On Stone.

A GATHERING OF BUFFALO

The buffalo roaming the fields of Gladie Creek are properly called bison. Their ancestral Asian immigrants migrated to North America, crossing the Bering Sea land bridge that once connected the two continents, probably during several periods of prehistory.

According to historical records, these hoofed mammals were reported to have been in this vicinity. In 1750 and 1751, both Dr. Thomas Walker and Christopher Gist reported seeing buffalo along what is now Red River during their travels. Daniel Boone and other "Long Hunters" observed buffalo during early exploration into Kentucky during the 1770's.

Buffalo have been credited as the first road makers in Kentucky. Usually, buffalo trails followed the line of least resistance from one water hole or salt lick to another. Grazing on the grass and foliage along the way, the cleared the underbrush. A popular misconception is that Indians used buffalo traces for thousands of years before the first European pioneers entered the area. Current archeological evidence indicates that buffalo did not reach Kentucky until about 300-400 years ago. During this period many of these traces became known as "Indian Roads". In fact, Red River was once known as the Warriors Fork. The early pioneers found these paths convenient travel routes because they almost invariably led to water. Many present-day highways in Kentucky follow original buffalo trails.

Overhunting and the conversion of open plains to settled farmland forced the decline of the buffalo from Kentucky. Most experts agree the last buffalo were in Kentucky around the early 1800's and had disappeared altogether by 1820. The restoration of the buffalo from near extinction to the present day numbers is truly one of the most dramatic conservation stories of the century.

Once again these magnificent beasts, who were once teetering on the brink of extinction, can quietly live out their life spans amid the spiney prominences of the Red River Gorge in the Daniel Boone National Forest. The return of buffalo to this site is the result of cooperative efforts of The Red River Wildlife Association, Clark Rural Electric Cooperative, and Forest Service, USDA.

THE LOGGING RAILROADS

On July 16, 1901 A.K. Sewell, 16 years old, was the fireman and Harry White the engineer on a logging locomotive. The rest of the train crew consisted of Alex McGregor, acting train foreman, and brakeman George Kelly, Marion Kelly, John Chapel and Jeff Taylor. William Montgomery, a friend of the crew, was apparently riding on the train.

A lawsuit filed over the death of A.K. Sewell on the above date alleged that Alex McGregor, who replaced the regular train foreman, John Warden, for this run, was inexperienced and incompetent to act in the capacity of train foreman. The lawyer for the deceased claimed that upon reaching a switch, the foreman and brakeman got off the train and the engineer started down the switch before the brakeman were able to climb aboard. Without the added braking power of the cars, the train quickly gained speed on a steep temporary track and derailed after running about 1200 feet, causing Sewell to be scalded to death and injured William Montgomery, the passenger. The lawyer also stated the engine was equipped with "chilled –face wheels." which were made for and intended only to be run on wooden rails and the road where the accident occurred had steel rails.

Wooden rails for temporary tram roads were used when it when it was not practical to lay steel rail. Construction was similar. Material, except for spikes, was already on hand. Hewn crossties or small logs were laid on a minimum graded surface and wood rails fastened to these ties with spikes. Wood rails were hardwood lengths, spiked together with overlapping cuts, using counter-sunk holes to prevent the spike heads from being above the rails.

Needless the say, the wooden tracks were temporary as they were intended to be. The purpose was removing timber not a passenger line.

THE DOG DROWNING HOLE

In the upper Red River Gorge, between Silvermine and Pecks Branch is an area known locally as the Dog Drowning Hole. This is a swirl of water with a downward suction.
A coon hunter and his dog were out one night on Red River pursuing the popular local
sport of coon hunting. Coons will often take to water when pursued by dogs, and this night was no exception. To shake off the dog, the coon plunged, whether by accident or design, right into the swirl of water and was immediately pulled under. The coon dog followed him and met the same fate. From that day forward, the swirl was known as the Dog Drowning Hole.

COW CAVE GAP

Cow Cave Gap is a break in the cliff near Sky Bridge, and was the main route used by early settlers to get from Red River to Pine Ridge. It was so named because a cow once fell into a crevice in the gap and nearly starved to death before it was discovered and rescued.

THE MILL HOLE

On Swift Camp Creek behind and upstream from the Sleepy Hollow Lodge is a spot known as the Mill Hole. According to old timers, there was at one time a water-powered gristmill located here. I have been unable to locate any trace of the mill by physical examination of the area or by research of maps and

records.   There exists, however, a strange unidentified "V"
shaped structure of concrete blocks in the area described as the
mill location. Dimensions are 10 feet long, 5 feet wide and
8 feet high, forming an apex at the east end.

THE NADA BAND MILL

While the Nada Tunnel was being constructed, the Dana Lumber Company was busy installing a large band sawmill at the newly established village of Nada. The settlement was located at Dana's logging spur junction with the L & E Railroad, slightly less than a mile east of old Lombard. The abandoned depot at Lombard (former junction of the Big Woods Lumber Company Railroad) was moved to the new location site of Nada. The origin of the name was an anagram of Dana. (Changing letter order).

The newly established community retained the old Lombard Post Office. Nada became the nucleus of the company's activity. In addition to the band sawmill and depot, there was a general store, boarding houses, lathe mill, storage buildings, blacksmith and locomotive shops, and a large air-drying lumber yard.

In 1914 a fire destroyed the sawmill. Dana never rebuilt, but leased its entire acreage and sold all its appurtenances to the Broadhead-Garret Company. The Broadhead family was residents of Pennsylvania, and H.G. Garret was a native lumberman with immense timber knowledge of the Gorge.

Between 1914 and 1920, the Broadhead-Garret Company launched the most massive timbering effort in the history of the gorge. Logs were floated by means of splash dams (see Splash Dam Primer) to a point near the mouth of Chimney Top Creek. A boom would catch and hold them. In turn, the log loader would hoist the logs onto flatcars, ready to be trained to the mill. Once the logs were sawed at the Nada mill they were stacked, air-dried and finally loaded on the main line railroad to be exported to distant markets.

In 1920, logging operations ceased and the mill was sold, dismantled and moved to Tennessee.

DANIEL BOONE IN THE RED RIVER GORGE

When Daniel Boone first came to Kentucky, he was 35 years old and had achieved little of special significance. Two of his three military campaigns had been failures, and although he had explored as far south as Florida, there was little to distinguish him from other explorers and hunters of the same period.

Daniel Boone was supposed to have spent a winter alone in this area, possibly in the crude wood and stone hut, which bears his name. (See D.Boon hut) Imagine what the Red River Gorge would have been like two centuries ago. To have seen what Daniel Boone must have. Boone was one of the most fascinating characters in Kentucky History. A Quaker by religion and wanderlust by trade, a man who was never satisfied until he crossed that next ridge.

Boone apparently hunted in the gorge area from 1769 to 1771. The finding of a hand-hewn roof shake with D. BooN stippled on it under a great cathedral of overhanging rock, in a remote of the gorge in 1968 touched off a debate that endures to this day. A laboratory analysis of the red oak shake indicated it was probably 200 years old, but also showed the carving had been added after the board had weathered. A well-preserved relic of the Boone era when Kentucky was still virtually unexplored with areas and distances unmeasured would by all accounts be of tremendous historic value. Whether the carving is authentic is questionable.

Historians hesitate to verify much about Boone. It has been over 200 years and few records were kept in those days. It is all but impossible to separate the legend from the truth, but he comes to us as a mixture of myth and reality. A man who certainly deserved better than he received in light of the role he played in opening the Kentucky frontier.

It is true he has his honors, but they were largely posthumously. In his final piece of earth, he finally had land that could not be taken away.

In 1966, the name of the Cumberland National Forest was changed to Daniel Boone National Forest to honor the man who was responsible for the settlement of Kentucky and subsequently the western expansion of the American Frontier. Boone's exploits as a backwoodsman and Indian fighter elevated him to folk hero status. Boone has become a kind of patriarch not only to Kentucky but also to the entire nation as an individual who symbolized the American frontier.

THE SHELTOWEE TRACE

The Sheltowee Trace was established in 1979 as a national recreation trail of the U.
S. Forest Service. Beginning near Morehead and about 30 miles south of the Ohio River, the trail links up with the Red River Gorge, a 30 square mile geological wonderland, reminiscent of the Grand Canyon in miniature. Sheltowee then zigzags southward through Kentucky before ending in Tennessee. Most of the 257 miles cross the Daniel Boone National Forest, honoring the famous woodsman. Sheltowee, meaning Big Turtle, was the name given to Boone by the Shawnee who captured and adopted him into the tribe. The adoption rites were apparently painful, as the hair on the head was plucked out by a tedious and painful operation, leaving a turf some three or four inches in diameter on the crown, for the scalp lock which is cut and dressed with feathers. Than Boone was taken to as river and there thoroughly washed and rubbed, "To take out all the white blood." The war chief, Blackfish, than adopted him into the tribe as his own son.

The Shawnees captured Boone in 1776 near Boons borough while hunting and scouting for the salt-making camp. (See Salt-Making) Boone, in a effort to save Boonsbourgh, led the Shawnees to the salt camp and persuaded the men to surrender.

A council was convened and for hours, the solemn debate proceeded, as warrior after warrior rose and spoke for mercy or death of the captives. Daniel Boone was permitted to make the closing speech. The war club passed from hand to hand as the vote was taken under the eyes of the captives. Fifty-nine warriors dashed it into the ground, as a vote for death; sixty-one let it pass as a token of mercy. There is a faint story the Indians let Boone vote.

RUSSIANS AND KENTUCKIANS AT GLADIE

On October 13, 1990 at the Gladie Creek Historic Site Sorghum Festival, a scheduled 32 member choral group from the Soviet Union arrived for a visit. They were treated to a traditional Kentucky dinner of chicken and dumplings, shuck beans, cornbread, and pumpkin pie. Coffee was served up from a two gallon blue granite coffee pot heated over an open fire.

When the meal was over, many of the group participated in the sorghum making and afterwards responded by singing several Russian folk songs in acappella chorus. Toward the end of the last number, a wonderful thing happened. In a spontaneous gesture of friendship, Russians and Kentuckians joined hands in an impromptu polka around the field.

What a historic event to happen! Right here at Gladie Creek, in Menifee County, Kentucky.

Russian woman feeding cane into sorghum mill with the help of Rondel Lee.

LAUREL FORK ROCK QUARRY

In Laurel Fork near Parched Corn Creek quietly stands a few concrete piers reminisce of the remains of a rock crusher and quarry. This area once hummed with activity as the rock was produced by the Civilian Conservation Corps for the various road building projects. Little is known of this site and the history is dim. The quarry is noted on a 1937 map of the Red River Ranger District, Cumberland National Forest. Pictured below is the original apparatus for crushing the rock at Laurel Fork. The second picture is of the quarry. Note workers.

PINE TAR INDUSTRY IN RED RIVER GORGE

Scattered throughout the Red River Gorge are the circular remains of earthen mounds heaped in mute testimony to yet another gorge industry: Pine tar pits.

The making of pine tar must have been practiced quite extensive as evidenced by the remains of these many depressions.

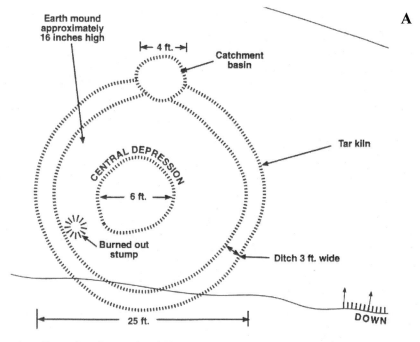

circular pit of varying diameter was dug and lined with clay. The dirt from the excavation was placed around the pit in a circular ring. Pitch Pine (fat pine, rich pine) was placed or piled in this pit, covered with dirt and set fire. As the pine burned in a sort of smothered combustion, the pitch oozed out, and settled to the hard packed clay bottom of the pit. The tar drained to the low side into a catch basin. A tar pit on Tunnel Ridge Road measures 25 feet across, with the central depression 6 feet across and 10 inches deep. The catch basin is on the downhill side and is about 4 feet in diameter and 16 inches deep. The mounded ring of earth is about 16 inches high. The ditch depression around the outer edge of the pit is 3 feet wide.

When just a small amount of tar was needed around a homestead, the process was somewhat different. A shallow groove was cut into the rock to allow the basin to drain. Pine was ricked up and a kettle (20 gallon was the preferred kind) was placed over the pine and sealed round the rim of the kettle to keep the flames from the fire to be built from going in under the rim and setting the pine inside on fire.
Wood was piled over the kettle and a fire started. It was necessary to keep a hot fire to melt down the pitch. When the tar melts, it starts to flow through the groove down the side of the rock and must be collected at that point.

The grooves cut into the rock for drainage are somewhat similar to the so-called "Peace Symbol" or Broken Cross.

The pine tar was used for medications, crude turpentine, wagon wheel hubs, and   when cattle were dehorned. For coughs, it was mixed with molasses and sulfur.

THE OLD GLADIE CEMETERY

One of the most permanent features of the Gladie community has been the cemetery, still quite visible today. Only one tombstone is readable. This is the grave of Alfred Hale, son of Mary Hale Nolan. Mary was the daughter of Levi Hale. Elijah Spencer who died on October 18, 1876, is probably one of the earliest burials at the Gladie cemetery documented to date. This early interment is intriguing and suggests some settlement by the Spencer's before the Ledford's arrived.

Two of the cemetery graves are those of a child of Rebecca Sargent (daughter of Aunt Sallie Sargent) and a child of Isie Helton (daughter of Jonathan, son of Thurston and Priscilla Helton). Her father Isaac, a brother to Jonathan helped make the little coffins and the bodies were carried up the river to the Gladie cemetery.

Other burials at the cemetery include Elizabeth/Ferbie Spencer Sargent, born in 1886 and died in 1902 reportedly after having fallen into a hog lot and being killed by the hogs. She was the wife of Bone Sargent. Bone Sargent's child, William Taylor Sargent, who died at 16 in 1902. Others include a child by the name of Robe Brown who died in the 1930's. The wife of "Old Ale" Ledford, the mother of Rusha Ledford Ratliff and Rebecca Gilbert. There is a possibility that John and Melina Ledford (parents of Joe B.Ledford) may also be buried here. In the 1900 census, Joseph B. Ledford's household includes not on himself and his wife Belle and their children, but also John, age 90 and Melina, age 71.

The last two interments may have been in 1917, when Jess and Vesta Ledford buried there after being killed in a car wreck. According to old timers, Jess and Vesta were moved to the Ledford cemetery at Pine Ridge in the 1930's. Something to do with the road going through the lower part of Gladie cemetery.

THE GLADIE SCHOOL

The school at Gladie is a prominent memory to many former residents, and must have been an important part of the community. How the land was obtained for the school lot is unclear. No deeds are on record that shows the Ledford's deeding school property to Menifee County. Jody Peck recalls his teachers at Gladie as having been Nellie Ledford, Frank Peck and Oscar Helton. Bill Profitt, who was listed as a student in 1926, remembered that the teacher that year was Nellie Gibbs. Other teachers include Corbett Peck and Stella Lawson.

A circa 1926 photograph of Gladie School shows a one room frame structure built on native rock piers, with Jewell Rock in the background. One former student observed the school was quite new when he was a student in 1912. The picture captures Stella Lawson with a group of pupils. They have been identified as follows: Billie Gibbs, son of Stanley and Nellie Gibbs, Pearl Ledford, who was staying with White Ledford at the Klaber house; a child of Saul Helton; Charlot Ledford (daughter of White Ledford); Joe Ledford (son of White Ledford); Basil Peck; Kate Hale (daughter of Dutch Hale);Carl Peck, Strother Hale (son of Dutch Hale); Eveline Peck, (son of White Ledford); Kelly Ledford (daughter of White Ledford); Charlie Hale (son of Dutch Hale); Bertha Long and Lennox Fletcher. A 1926 listing of school children gives a grouping of five families, those headed by White Ledford, Dutch Hale, Jeff Profitt, Dillard Profitt and Stanley Gibbs. Other children listed in this document but not present in the school photo include Lillie Mae Ledford, Willard Hale, Frank Hale, Willie Profitt and Nora Profitt.

The school is reported to have been torn down in the late 1930's and the material used to build the frame house at Pumpkin Bottom, which exists today.

THE KLABER HOUSE

Klaber Branch is the second branch of Gladie Creek from Red River on the Northwest side. This house, a large log structure, was probably built between 1894 and 1898. Sam Quinlin stated in an Affidavit he helped Joseph Klaber build the house in 1894. A. Nolan, another local person, recalls the date as 1898. These dates are substantiated by the fact Joseph Klaber bought property in this area in 1893, from James and Minerva Ledford. The deed calls the stream Tillman Branch. However, nothing is known of Tillman ownership or occupation and the name is not listed in the 1880 census.

The Klabers held the property until 1914, when they sold to Broadhead-Garret. The family was large in 1900 and included Jacob (age 43), wife Julia F. (38), children, Elizabeth (18), Jacob Jr., (16), Gracie (13), Abbie (10), Freddie (6), Hattie (4), Earl (2), Myrtle (8), Sherlie (two mo), and Willie (24). The U.S. Post Office records list Julia F. Klaber as Postmaster at Gladie from 1902-1905.

White Ledford with wife (Stella Tackett Ledford) and family lived in the house for a time. They moved to Chimney Top after being washed out in a flood. Part of the house is visible in the photograph below. The other photograph shows Fred Klaber (on horse) at a logging operation on Red River.

DUTCH HALE

Hale Branch, up from Klaber is so named because of Levi Hale's house. His son, Dutch and Wife Evie also lived nearby. Dutch was a railroad tie maker and carpenter. He sometimes stayed in the lumber camps, coming back to his home on weekends. According to old timers, the house was two to three rooms. The family eventually moved to Tarr Ridge and was mostly wiped out by tuberculosis. Just opposite the Dutch Hale house, was a long 3-room log house where the Pecks lived. Mrs. Peck was a daughter to Levi and a sister to Dutch. All three families living in the area were Hales. Old timers remember Levi Hale with a long white beard and wearing a black suit and white shirt.

DUTCH AND EVIE HALE WITH FAMILY

SON OF DEVIL SAL

At a small church in the Red River Gorge, a preacher was rapping out an intense sermon, when he noted a young man entering the door. "Young man, he thundered, are you looking for SALvation. No, came the firm reply, I am looking for Sal Sargent." Lize Sargent was the son of Devil Sal Sargent. Lize formerly lived in Sargent's Branch, which was home to the Sargent family. Lize left his wife and moved up on Swift Creek where he married a second time.

Sargent's branch was once known as Pelfrey Hollow. The 1900 census s list the family of William F. and Mary V. Pelfrey at Gladie.

JEWEL ROCK

Jewell Rock is visible from the old Gladie School site, and was named after Blue Jewell. He is listed in the 1900 census as being born in 1872. According to the story, Blue built a rudimentary ladder to the top of the rock in order to pick the huckleberries growing there. He lived in various places up and down Red River.

Today the area is known as Jewel Pinnacle and is a popular rock climbing area.

CCC SIDE CAMP

A CCC camp was established at Frenchburg in 1934, and during the later years of this program, Stanley and Nellie Gibbs house at Gladie was used as a side camp, with a focus on roadwork in the gorge. The Gibbs moved into a cabin near the chicken house. A 6 hole toilet for the CCC workers was perched on the edge of the bank. There was also a shop set near the electric pole, where they kept tools and supplies.

LEDFORDS AND LOGGING

The earliest documented involvement of the Ledford's in logging comes from court testimony that Ale Ledford cut about 100 logs in the right fork of Chimney Top creek in 1887 for Captain Thomas and Company. This is the same Thomas of the early Red River Lumber Mills, which went into business at Clay City around 1877.

According to court testimony in 1890 a B.A. Sexton was hauling logs for Stephen Bordens and A.C.Ledford, these logs to be turned over to the Center Lumber Company (formed 1880), who in turn sold to the Kentucky Union Company.

Joseph B. Ledford left the Red River for a time to run a hotel on McCausey. This venture may have been prompted by his experience in running a boarding house at Gladie Creek. This venture must not have been to his liking, for he sold to Shelly Connoy in February, 1900.

In 1917, Joseph Ledford was in control of over 4000 acres along Red River, Gladie, Chimney Top and Wolfpen Creeks, property which he held until 1937 when he deeded the Gladie area to his daughter, Nellie Ledford Gibbs, who had married

Stanley Gibbs, in 1918, a close friend of her brother Floyd Ledford from WWI.

Joe and his wife, Belle settled down near the mouth of Chimney Top Creek, in the shadow of Chimney Rock in 1922 and built a small house. This was near the site of the "Great Log Boom" across Red River that caught and held the logs. A log loader would hoist the logs onto flatcars. The remains of this boom are visible today with grooves worn into the rock and bits of rusted wire rope.

In 1933, Joseph and Belle built another house of substantial size a short distance away from the first one. He hired Sam Quinlan, Jim Tabor and Charlie Hill for this task. He resided here 14 years. This was a two story frame structure consisting of three bedrooms and a bathroom upstairs and a living room, dining room and kitchen downstairs, covering 1562 sq. ft.

He died in this house on April 17, 1947 two weeks away from being 87 years old. Joseph and Belle are buried at the Lovelace Cemetery in Menifee County.

CCC IN RED RIVER GORGE

The remains of the Pine Ridge Civilian Conservation Corps camp are located along both sides of KY 715 about one mile north from the junction of KY 15. The camp was designated as F-1 (the number given by the state to the project and camp), Company 1559V. (The number given by the federal government to each company"V" stands for veterans meaning the camp was comprised of veterans of World War I. The camp was first occupied on July 19, 1933 and completed December 15, 1933.The camp opened with 115 men and had expanded to 222 men by August 25, 1934. Captain Philip Porter was in command and Lieutenant James Stamper as the second in command. Lieutenant Frank Alexander was the camp doctor while Peter Gearhart was Project Superintendent for the Forest Service.

From the date the camp was established to July 25, 1934, the following work was reported: 40 miles of telephone line completed, 12 miles of roadside clearing. Erected 2 steel lookout towers and another 50% complete. Erected two lookout cabins. Spent 500-man day's forest fire fighting, 750 days on fire presuppression and 150 days on fire prevention. Completed 22 miles of truck trails, erected one equipment depot and six-room dwelling. Erected 1 tool house, 1 office building and 28 toolboxes. Erected two explosive magazines, and a stone crusher plant. Painted three lookout towers and five buildings.

A newsletter was published bi-monthly focusing on camp activity and was known as the Pine Ridge Peckerwood, later changed to Red River Peckerwood. One night was set aside for entertainment of the families of enrollees who lived nearby. Fondly named "The Wood Hens" referring of course to the "Mrs. Veterans" who provided an interested and enthusiastic audience.

 By July 22, 1935, the Pine Ridge Camp had been moved to Bowen Kentucky keeping the same Company Number of 1559V, but now designated as F-9. What prompted this move is somewhat obscure; however, there were some problems with the Pine Ridge Camp. Heating in winter was inadequate. The bathhouse had only four showerheads to serve 222 enrollees. The lighting was obtained from a Crocker Wheeler unit of 5 KW however, this was not always reliable as there was no backup generator and the refrigeration units were too small. Another problem may have been moonshine whiskey. There was plenty of moonshine in the vicinity and a statement from one of the camp officers was "the hardest thing to contend with in the line of discipline is drinking." To prevent the sale of moonshine in the camp, there were two night guards and several key men who were under orders to notify the camp commander of any suspected bootleggers. There were a number of complaints and many discharges of enrollees due to drunkenness. Other discharges included abuse of government equipment, continuous agitation, lagging and shirking on the job and refusal to abide by camp regulations.

By June 30, 1934 a newly appointed Camp School Adviser, former senior foreman John Martin, launched an active program of classes and activities for Pine Ridge. They included math, elementary and advanced English, music, forestry, civics, agriculture, first aid, shorthand and cooking.

Two more camps were established in the general vicinity. One camp was established at Natural Bridge State Park on November 18, 1933, Project SP-2, Company 567 in Powell County. The other was established near Frenchburg at Becky Jane Hollow in Menifee County, Project F-8, Company 1539 on October 3, 1934.

An evaluation project is in the planning stages to promote community involvement, and identify the remains of the numerous buildings which occupied the site of the Pine Ridge CCC Camp. The drilled and cased well has been located along with barracks sites and bathhouse. Two large raised earthen ramps which may have served as "grease racks", components of a cistern system, the camp commissary and officers quarters (first picture). The labor focus was one of roads and bridges. Note Red River Bridge construction above.

On the south side of Kentucky Route 715, in the late 1950's was the site of a picnic area with four tables, outdoor toilet and parking lot. Appropriately signed as the Old Campground, the facilities were removed about 1970. They were located close to the site of the officer's quarters at the old Pine Ridge CCC Camp.

It is hoped this CCC site will be further evaluated in order to interpret and enhance this old camp. On June 30, 1943, the

CCC camps were abolished by an act of congress. The Pine Ridge Camp left its mark, and relics of dedicated service are scattered over the vicinity. This should not be allowed to become a mere footnote in history. The old camp had its day then faded into long years of oblivion, but could be revived as a modern day attraction.

IN THE SHADOW OF CHIMNEY ROCK

Chimney Rock, a convoluted monolith of stone, has stood sentinel over the gorge since time and erosion created this grand cathedral of nature. If the rock could speak, what tales could unfold! From the ancients who camped beneath the curve of the shadow, to producing a world famous female folk singer, Chimney Rock has stood as a lookout of the times and reckoned prominently in local history.

There is some indication Chimney Rock and the stream below were named by Powell Rose. It is said that Rose witnessed the fall of the many boulders that surround the old house site. Rose apparently settled the area around 1840 and was an established resident when he created one of the first enterprises in the Red River Gorge, a business known as the "boat yard." Here he constructed barges of native white oak, filled them with coal and floated the ensemble to Frankfort were he disposed of the entire load including the boat. He than faced a long walk home.

Lily May Ledford was a gifted young musician who came out of eastern Kentucky in response to the opportunity created by radio in the 1920;s and 30's. She was a great success at Chicago's WLS National Barn Dance and at Renfro Valley Barn Dance. As a member of the famous "Coon Creek Girls," the first all-woman band, she toured the Southeast, sang for the King and Queen of England by invitation of President Franklin Roosevelt and performed on Broadway.

She was born in the Red River Gorge beneath the shadow of Chimney Rock on March 17, 1917 to Daw White Ledford and Stella May Ledford. White Ledford rented his land from Joe B. Ledford, who built the first modern style house in the gorge around 1933.

Between 1914 and 1920 Broadhead and Garrett Lumber
Company launched the most massive timbering effort in the
history of the gorge. Logs were floated by means of splash dams
to a point near the mouth of Chimney Top Creek where they
were caught by "the great log boom." stretched across Red
River. A log
Loader would hoist the logs onto train cars for their journey to
the mill.

In the 1930's the Federal Government began buying land in the
gorge area for National forest purposes. In 1937 the area was
proclaimed the Cumberland National Forest. In 1966
Cumberland was changed to Daniel Boone to honor that great
pioneer who served Kentucky so well.

Throughout the years Chimney Rock, from its lofty eminence,
has looked out over the changing seasons of inhabitants. From
early man who carved his message on the sandstone boulders, to
other men who carved their message of remorse (see Chronicles
on the Rock), Pine Tar Kilns, Saltpeter extraction, Railroads, all
played their part, lived their hour and left behind names that
will endure as long
as there is a Red River Gorge.

The gorge is now experiencing a new boom –tourism. Visitors
are coming for the same reason as yesterday's natives stayed.
Therefore, in a sense we have come full circle. Just as the
geological spender awed early man, so is the visitor today
amazed at the natural phenomenon.

As well they may, visitors have known the Red River Gorge
contains both intangible and tangible assets: beauty, solitude,
naturalness, wild abundance, deep hollows, bizarre rock
formations, and rough-hewn cliff lines. It is among this
naturalness that about 250 natural arches exist, quietly living
out their life spans among the towering cliffs.

A few great moments and people from the shadow of Chimney Rock-

THE CEDAR THICKET

A famous former resident of the Red River Gorge told this story to me many years ago. This is how she related it:

Deep in the Red River Gorge near Gladie Creek, there once stood a small two-room shack secluded by a large cedar thicket. In this house, there lived a man and his wife many, many years ago. This man was reputed to have a sadistic temper and would often beat his wife. Her screams could be heard throughout the hollow where they lived. Suddenly there came a time when the screams were heard no more by the neighbors and the woman had not been seen by anyone for some time. Curious neighbors began to question the man concerning his wife's whereabouts and he appeared very nervous. Finally, he replied, 'why she died of the flu and I buried her out there in the cedar thicket.' After telling this story, the man disappeared and was never seen again. The local folks having their suspicions aroused, searched for the cedar thicket and did in fact find a recent earth disturbance. They decided to dig at this spot and soon struck a wooden oblong box made of rough lumber. Prying off the lid of the box, even the strongest man present was horrified. For there in the box lay the wife! She had turned over in the rough box and had torn the hair out of her head. Her hands were full of it. Her fingertips were bloody stubs with the nails torn out. Long scratches were everywhere on the lid of her tomb. The man had beaten his wife unconscious and buried her alive.

The cedar thicket where this tragedy happened is known as The Cedar Thicket to this day and is passed by many hikers of the Sheltowee Trace unaware of the calamity, which occurred here yesteryear.

THE INDENTURED SERVANT

An indenture is a legal contract binding one party into the service of another for a specified term. In the case of an indentured servant, the term is usually seven years, after which time the servant earns his freedom. It is actually a form of slavery.

On the top of a high cliff, overlooking the Band Mill Bottom on Indian Creek, there is a carving, which is, reminisces of an English man. The carving is reputed to have been done by an indentured servant on Tarr Ridge who sorely missed his native country. The English features are apparent. Note the closed eyes and uplifted chin. The story goes this servant would walk to the edge of the cliff where the green stream bottom reminded him of his homeland. He began to carve out on the rock a face with features of his compatriots as a reminder of his domicile.

This work of rock art is gone now. Forever destroyed by a careless campfire built directly on top of this feature.

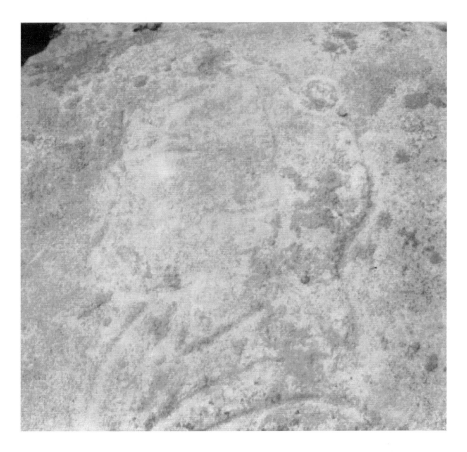

Many such features are destroyed by the careless acts of
humankind. From ancient petroglyphs to saltpeter works, the
destruction has been indiscriminate. Whether it is a do not
know or don't care attitude the results are the same. We do
have a connection with the past. If we continue to destroy
artifacts, we may lose the strand that links us to the past. And in
so doing, could easily lose our way by destroying the landmarks
from which we take our bearings

RIVER MEN

When logs were being floated down the Red River to Clay City, they were herded along much like a cattle drive, by river men instead of cowboys. Armed with Pike Poles instead of 45 revolvers, the river man's job was to keep the logs moving in the water and avoid logjams. The Pike Poles were usually in three lengths; twelve, fourteen and sixteen feet. However, the fourteen-foot pole was not widely used. On the end of the pole was a spike and hook. Serving double duty, the spike was used to push and the hook to pull the lodged logs. They were also used for balancing when the river man jumped from log to log, reminiscent of the balance rod of a high wire walker. Many loggers wore small spikes in both the heel and toe of their boots. Others preferred the heel spikes only.

Two river men of the Red River Gorge log drive days were Marcus Potts, and Johnny McCutcheon. It is said that Marcus Potts could roll a log until the water splashed over his head. This was known in river jargon as "cutting the log." He could nimbly walk across the river jumping from log to log. The trick is using your toes and leaving the logs quickly. Potts had spikes in the heel of his boots only, saying he could negotiate the logs easier without spikes in the toes. He preferred the log jumping between booms instead of walking along the banks.

Johnny McCutcheon was reputed to have weighed over 300 pounds. The man, as big as he was, could get around on a log. He could select a log and ride out in the water anywhere he wanted. Freeing logjams was his specialty.

PROLOGUE TO SAGA OF AN ARCH

Sky Bridge is old in geologic time. As ageless as it may seem the bridge has a life span that in some ways is comparable to that of a living being. The same erosion process that created Sky Bridge will bring about its demise. When an arch is young, it has many rough edges and is usually very strong. At the onset of maturity, differential weathering has smoothed out the rough edges, creating symmetry without a significant loss of strength. When an arch reaches old age it usually well rounded with slender graceful lines, but by this time it has become weakened by the constant bombardment of the erosion process, taking on a sand-blast like appearance, which in effect it is. Due to this natural order, arches will eventually collapse and die, just as living beings do.

The lifespan of an arch depends upon how resistant to weathering the parent material from which it was formed. Strength depends upon the shape of the arch and the type of rock formation. The fabricated arch in many construction projects is strong because it is subjected to compression. The strongest shape of all is the Inverted Catenary due to this compression principle. Flat Iron Arch is a good example of such natural architecture.

In the Saga of an Arch epistle, the reader will find a bond between the arch and humankind related in the imaginary words of Sky Bridge articulating. In this mythical discussion the arch laments the passing of it's time as do we all. From a lofty perch on the dividing ridge between Parched Corn and Swift Creek overlooking the Red River, the arch observes man's inhumanity to man and a wide variety of social injustice down though the ages.

SAGA OF AN ARCH

My name is Sky Bridge. I am what is known in human jargon as a ridge top arch. There are many neighboring arches around, which are similar, yet different from me. They are called today by diverse names and are formed in several ways. Some of the types of arches I have heard about are cave, pothole, buttress, fin, pillar, bridging and of course ridge top.

However, I am getting ahead of my story.

I can vaguely remember the time of my birth. At the close of the Paleozoic Era (about 225 million years ago), this area was uplifted during the Appalachian Orogeny. The record thereafter was one of erosion. By Cretaceous time (about 100 million years ago), a peneplain had developed. Subsequent uplift during Tertiary time (less the 70 million years ago) resulted in a plateau of dendrite drainage's with a maze of irregularly winding narrow-crested ridges and deep narrow valleys. The effects of erosion and mass wasting created geomorphic conditions, principally narrow sandstone ridges, particularly suitable for the formation of arches.

Just before my birth, I was a long narrow ridge overlooking a river on a divide between two smaller streams. Here I was subject to weathering, erosion and mass wasting. Slowly at first, then more rapidly small sandstone blocks, formed by bedding planes were detached from the underside of the ridge and moved down slope by gravity. Erosion under mining of my less resistant underlying strata also contributed to the detachment. I must not forget the wind. If seems as if the wind was always blowing, moving minute grains of sand in a scouring type effect along my surface.

After an untold number of years, I had developed into a sort of shallow cave or what is known as a ROCKSHELTER. Then one fine day erosion forced an opening from the opposite side of the ridge. Very tiny to be sure, but at last light was passing completely through the ridge. I had become a LIGHTHOUSE. I stayed in this stage for many years while the forces of differential weathering enlarged the opening.

I cannot recall the exact time I passed from a lighthouse to an ARCH. The change was gradual and almost imperceptible, but I could feel a slight wearing away of my surface, but could not feel any significant loss of strength. Oh, it was great to be young, glorying in my power, holding aloft an enormous span of rock above, in a configuration that would much later be copied by man to hold large masses by the compression principle— what is known as an arch.

For what seems a long time after this I gradually began to feel a wearing away and weakening of my surface. It was sometime during this period that I became an object of awe and wonder to the first humans I ever met. To these people, now known as early or ancient man, I was a part of them sharing a common spirit.
I can remember ceremonies under the curve of my arch. At this time, I took no particular notice, but in retrospect, I noted these early people appeared to have a great respect for the land. The land and the ancients were one, each dependent upon the other.

Then came a time when I was alone again. The ancients had disappeared and I watched over a valley devoid of human life. In the meantime, my surface was still flaking, scoured by the wind, water and temperature changes. I guess by now I would be considered a mature arch.

I observed over the valley and noted the Indians came again. The numbers who visited me continued to grow over the years, and many began to live here the year round. I remember when they started planting small plots of squash, sunflower and goosefoot and asking me for a bountiful crop. Then the first members of the white race appeared upon my domain, and I witnessed my first major conflict between humans.

Something called War!

The Indians disappeared again, and I began to see small clearings or farms scattered sparsely around the area. Then something started to happen which I could not understand. The stately forest around me commenced to fall and there were many people, some with long sharp limber objects, who caused this fall. What a noise these trees made as they crashed to the ground! The river below floated the logs out, and on almost every stream of any size, a dam was constructed to hold back the water until sufficient volume was available to move the logs down to the river. Later, I witnessed the building of roads, and than one of the strangest sights, I had ever seen: That of a huffing, puffing, steel apparition on tracks that removed the logs and hauled them away.

I began to see more white settlers and their farms were scattered loosely over the area. Sometime during this period, I started to receive visitors. Someone called me the BIG LIGHTHOUSE and this name stuck for a period. Later, I was called SKY BRIDGE. I liked the name and it has endured to this day. During this time, I extolled in my slender graceful lines, and the image I must have portrayed from the valley floor. I was receiving thousands of visitors and was glad for the company.

After so many years of being exposed to the elements, I am aging. Millions of visitors have tramped across my spine loosening tiny grains of sand that gradually go deeper and deeper, Many thoughtless humans have carved their names or initials deep into my surface and on practically every vacant spot, thus hastening my demise. In fact, I believe I have suffered the loss of more surface material during the past 50 years than I have in the previous 5000 years.

I have grown old and am in the winter of my life. The constant stream of visitors is welcome, but I have become tired of the traffic. I have seen so many people who toss their trash carelessly about my surface. Some have even sprayed paint on

128

me then a cleanup crew tries to remove the paint and in the process takes a part of my surface with it. I can ill afford the loss at this stage of my life. Other people get too close to my edge and plunge to the rocks below. I have heard it said I should be fenced on each edge of my spine. I shudder to think what would happen if postholes were drilled into my already weakened surface.

A few rare times I am alone with my memories. But they are magnificent memories. I remember the great plateau, the age-long sculpturing of my form, and the first people who came to visit me. I remember glorying in my youth, and what a fine figure I was at that time. I remember how I was once an object of worship, held in awe and wonder, and now how people think nothing of cutting deeply into my surface, tossing trash or spraying paint. Such hurt and humiliation!

During my final time, I can only hope that people will once again respect the land. If you are walking across my spine, consider all the arches, and look upon our ageless struggle with the elements and do not hasten our fall. Please do not desecrate our surface with trash, carving and spray paint. I understand you are probably reaching out with an unconscious quest for immortality, but do not be deceived. All things must pass. We all have our moments, the spring summer autumn and winter of our lives.

So here am I, overlooking the valley below and the Red River. I am told the rivers sometimes rejuvenate themselves and become young again. I sometimes wish this could happen to me.

I dimly remember, someone saying one windy day from the top of my spine, some words over which I have often pondered. I believe he called it a Psalm and it goes something like this: "As for man, his days are as grass; as a flower of the field, so he flourisheth. For the wind passeth over it, and it is gone; and the place thereof shall know it no more."

Is this all there is for man? Will it be thus for me?

129

I wonder.

LILY MAY LEDFORD 1917-1985

Lily May Ledford is a true Kentucky legend, best remembered for having led America's first all girl string band, the Coon Creek Girls. She is considered to have been one of the best self-taught banjo players, and was an accomplished all around musician.

She was a natural for performing, loved to really "cut loose" for an audience, and had a charming personality to boot. This, along with her exceptional musical abilities, made her feel right at home on the stage. Audiences loved to be entertained by her authentic old time music.

Lily May was born right here in the Red River Gorge on March 27, 1917 over on Chimney Top Creek, near Pinch-Em-Tight Gap. For a while, her family lived at Klaber Branch off Gladie Creek but moved farther downriver when all their crops washed away in a flood. She also lived at the restored Gladie Cabin off and on for extended periods. Pictured at left is a family photograph circa 1921. Front row -Rosie, White (seated) Lily Mae, Stella (seated) Coyen (infant) and Custer. Back row- Joe, Pearl and Kelly.

She was one of 14 children born to White and Stella Ledford, and regarded her childhood as a good and happy one. While growing up Lily May helped her family farm these narrow bottomlands. When she was working in the fields, she and her brothers and sisters would climb the steep hills to pick huckleberries and dig ginseng. She once said of her home in the

Gorge, "These are the prettiest, plushest, greenest hills anywhere. Photo to the left is Stella Ledford, circa 1921

She held many fond memories of her early years, especially the evenings when her family would sit around a fire roasting potatoes and chestnuts, listening to her father play the fiddle.

When the Ledford's acquired a banjo, little six-year-old Lily May picked it up and began playing right away. In fact, the whole family went crazy over that banjo until they finally wore it out. After that, there was not a lot of music making going on. Therefore, Lily May strung an old inner tube string between a green willow stick, and before long, she was plucking out tunes on her impromptu invention. It was somewhat of an unusual and crude instrument, but at least she could play her music again. Pictured left to right are Rosie, Lily Mae, Pearl Buchart (niece), Coyen, Custer, Kelly and Joe.

Then one day while picking poke greens, Lily May met up with a boy carrying an old beat up fiddle. She immediately knew she must have that fiddle, and traded several worldly possessions for it. Her next step was to make a bow, keys and bridge. Lily May could not have been happier. She would sneak off into the woods with the fiddle during chore time and hide way out in the woods on a hill behind a big rock where no one could find her, and just play for hours.

As a teenager, Lily May was getting to be a good player, performing at square dances and church meetings. Before long, she was entering and winning contests along with her brother Coyen, who was an excellent player. Eventually, the Red River Ramblers formed, consisting of Lily May, Coyen, their sister Rosie, and a neighbor, Morgan Skidmore.

At age 19, Lily May's career took off when she won a contest at Mount Vernon, Kentucky, and a spot on a radio program out of Chicago called the National Barn Dance. She also signed a five-year contract with agent, John Lair. Mr. Lair nurtured and encouraged her, telling her at one point not to change her mountain girl image. She was a real hit with her audience, and became known as the Kentucky Mountain Girl. That is exactly what she was, the real thing, and proud of her mountain heritage.

After Chicago, it was on to Cincinnati, where the Coon Creek Girls were born. The original band consisted of Lily May, Rosie Ledford, Esther or Violet Koehler, and Evelyn or Daisy Lange. Esther and Evelyn had decided to adopt new stage names to continue the flower theme with Lily and Rosie.

They played on the Renfro Valley Barn Dance program in Cincinnati for a while. In 1939, a highlight for the girls was a performance at the White House for President and Mrs. Roosevelt and King George VI and Queen Elizabeth.

Next, the Coon Creek Girls began performing at the all-new Renfro Valley in Rockcastle County, Kentucky. Then, Violet and Daisy left the band after getting married. Now the band was Lily May, Rosie, and Minnie or Black-eyed Susie, another Ledford sister. They continued performing on the barn dance program off and on for 18 years, and even performed in a

show on Broadway where they were very well received. Eventually the band broke up in 1957, because the women, all married, were busy raising their children. Lily May herself had three talented children, Barbara, Jimmy and Bobby.

In the 1960's and 70's, Lily May saw a renewed interest in folk music, particularly on college campuses. She, and oftentimes her sisters, had the opportunity to play at folk festivals and schools all around the country and abroad. She continued to enjoy performing in the years that followed, and in 1979 and 1980, she was Berea College Artist in Residence, performing and giving seminars. In 1983, she recorded an album called "Lily May Ledford Banjo Picking Girl." In 1985, a month before she passed on, she received the National Endowment for the Arts Heritage Award.

Therefore, we honor her here at The Gladie Creek Historic Site and celebrate her life and her music in remembrance and song. We hope Lily May approves.

THE HOUSE OF TAL

At the end of Calaboose Road in an area near the Roundabout, is a large native hand-cut sandstone chimney stark against the sky. This chimney stands like a giant cenotaph to the memory of a man who was among the first employees of the Red River Ranger District. If you should go to this area, do not look for the House of Tal, for it is no longer there. Time and weather have taken their toil so that only the chimney remains.

Tal Branham built the house about 1922 and the chimney was constructed by Henry Centers. A masterful piece of work, the chimney contains a double back-to-back fireplace that opened into the living room and parlor. In addition to these rooms, there was also a hallway, one bedroom and a kitchen and dining room. The living room and parlor doubled as bedrooms, two beds in each. The house was box frame, unpainted board and batten with two porches. The fireplace was situated near the center of the house, which faced the road.

Tal Branham lived here for many years raising a family. He worked for a time with the newly established Cumberland National Forest, the Red River Ranger District as a fire patrolman. He left the house about 1940 moving his belongings in a horse-drawn wagon teamstered by J.T. Spencer.

Enos Bailey, a local Wolfe County resident, rented the Tal House from 1940 to 1942. The old house was never occupied again after Enos moved out of the area.

The house, as with all abandoned houses, suffered the ravage of weather and rapidly aged due to lack of care until it finally collapsed leaving the work of art chimney exposed. I can remember the house still standing in the early 1960's along with a poplar log barn. Gone now. Over the changing seasons, only the rock remains the same.

The place is now part of the Clifty Wilderness. The U.S. Government in the year 2000 purchased the property from the Tal Braham heirs.

Tal is buried in the Tolson Cemetery near Harvest Time Chapel in Wolfe County.
He was born on September 25, 1895 and died on February 8, 1977, an eventual life full of years.

CHIMNEY VIEWS

CAMPTON AND HER SURROUNDINGS

(THE HAZEL GREEN HERALD) JUNE 17, 1885

Campton is situated on Swift's Camp Creek – not on one side, but on both – and was originally called "Swiftsville". It has three blacksmith shops and men to run them, one cabinet-maker, some few carpenters, one brick mason, plasterer and painter; some "Jacks-of-all-trades," 3 lawyers, 3 doctors, one hotel and 4 boarding houses, 5 stores, some 2 or 3 licensed preachers who never preach, but sometimes go to church, a steam-flour-and-corn mill, a Masonic hall, a Methodist church, a court-house partly finished, and a pen called a jail where the weary men sometimes find that which makes them feel happy, and if they can't find 'happiness' there our merchants kindly furnish them with "Strengthening Cordial," Hostetter's Bitters, Holland gin, etc. Then too, we have a police judge, a full board of trustees, and a town marshal, and not any more loafers than any other town of equal size will furnish, but will place her alongside of any town in Eastern Kentucky for cats, dogs and hogs.

However, I can say one thing for Campton, and few towns can make the same assertion truthfully, since its incorporation 25 years ago, there has been only one person killed in its limits and that during the war and by soldiers. While other places have dark and bloody spots that their citizens turn away from in ghostly horror, Campton is as pure and unspotted as ever the fresh-fallen snow.

I had forgotten to say we have measles in abundance and all their glory.

Only a little more than half a mile North of town begins the famous pine belt of Eastern Kentucky, and away to the north and west for miles stretches this vast pine forest. Here the spruce, the white and yellow pines, in all their native majesty, rears their towering branches toward Heaven. As yet this belt of timber is almost untouched. With the coming of the Kentucky Union railroad, this now almost worthless uninhabited section will be worth hundreds of thousands of dollars. About 6 miles north of Campton and in this pine belt, is the celebrated Swift's or Timmins' silver mine, the ores from which have been tested, and said to contain both gold and silver, while to the east and south of Campton abounds as fine forest of oak and poplar as can be found in Eastern Kentucky. Only four miles south of town is the celebrated Hobbs coal bank, 7 feet in thickness, which is pronounced by Prof. Proctor to be one of the finest coking coals in the world. Yet all this vast wealth of timber, of coal, of iron, must await the coming of capitalists and of transportation. Our people are generous and freehearted, and will gladly welcome any one whom desires to visit this section and see for themselves. Give, oh! Give us the Kentucky Union railroad, and instead of being a pauper county, we can then hold up our heads with the proudest of them.

Our farmers are busy working in their crops. Corn is rather small and wheat not good.

WOLFPEN CREEK

About 1905 Horton and Chester bought the timber on Wolfpen Creek. While in the process of removing the timber H&C built and operated storehouses, boarding houses and other houses as living quarters for their employees. Later, Joseph B. Ledford bought this property.

According to old-timers, there were several houses in the vicinity, long before the H&C buildings. Joe Ledford himself lived in the Wolfpen area as a tenant around 1890. He recalls an old house about a mile or more up Wolfpen Branch that was lived in and known as the Becky Moore house. Remains of the old house and orchard are visible today. There is also a cemetery with unmarked stone, said to be the grave of Becky Moore.

The old road into Wolfpen Creek follows the narrow gauge railroad grade of Broadhead and Garrett. In 1941, T.J. Gilbert of Winchester, Kentucky leased the oil and gas in this area, later leased in 1948 by Fred Crate Rice of Paintsville, Kentucky. In 1959, D. Nealy of Bay City, Texas drilled for oil to a depth of 1000 feet. According to Floyd Ledford, a local resident, this was a dry hole.

According to local legend, Wolfpen was so named because of traps set to capture a wolf, which was wrecking havoc with pigs in the area. This was supposedly the last wolf killed in the area.

EDWARDS (EDDARDS) BRANCH

During the logging days, Edwards Branch contained a large amount of valuable timber and a railroad was built along this branch from the grade on the south side of Red River near Fish trap. This project involved not only laying the rails, but also building a fordable crossing (unlike most railroads which used trestles) across Red River at the mouth of Edwards Branch. The remains of this crossing may be seen today underneath the water. The tracks have been long removed and even the old grade is obscure.

One of the last residents of the area was Rollie Denniston who lived with his wife and child at the forks of the stream. Another was Levi Stapleton. Many of the old-timers call the tributary Eddards Branch. The origin of the name Edwards Branch is lost to history.

The Dana Lumber Company purchased in 1909 over two thousand acres of timberland which included Edwards Branch. Dana's track gauge differed from the other lines in the area by being standard gauge (56 ½ inches wide) instead of narrow gauge (36 inches wide). In 1913 Dana entered into an agreement with R.L. Sullivan and Company to log Edwards Branch at a price of $5.50 per thousand feet delivered within 60 feet of the railroad.

Barn at Edwards Branch with Ed Hale holding mules during the logging days.

ENGINEERING THE CLIMAX ENGINE

Robert McNabb was an engineer on No. 2 Climax for Dana Lumber Company in the early 1900's hauling timber from the Grays Branch area to Dana's mill at Nada.

The Climax engine was designed to work in the steep, rugged slopes and had two engines that ran off the central boiler, which were powered by the boiler. When the train was going up steep grades the engines were used alternately, switching from one engine to the other by changing gears. The engines were connected to the drive wheels by gears.

Some of the grades were so steep that only five cars of logs could be hauled and it took two locomotives to do that.

One night on a run, McNabb's locomotive wheels slipped off the track, the train started sliding and turned over into Indian Creek. McNabb got out by climbing onto the trains running board. Engineers and train crews often learned the danger of logging in the gorge first hand.

POWDER MILL BRANCH

Powder Mill Branch is located behind the old house site of Shelby Palmer (individual who built the Indian Creek School) off Indian Creek in Menifee County. A Guide to Kentucky name places list no less than six Powder Mill Branches. As the name implies, these were sites of local powder mill where saltpeter from the rockshelter was converted to gunpowder.

Powder Mill Branch in Menifee County is referenced in several old deeds. In fact, the right fork was once known as Lead Branch. According to old timers, the lead seam was about a foot thick and located near the cliff line.

Niter was processed from the rock shelter saltpeter (See from Rockshelter to Gun barrel for a description of the process), ground and mixed with charcoal and sulfur to produce a crude form of gunpowder. The standard mixture was 75% niter, 15 % charcoal and 10% sulfur. As is apparent, niter is one of the prime ingredients in gunpowder. The ingredient ratio determines the explosive force of the powder.

An 1870 document provides this description. "One must pulverize separately 76 parts of nitrate and possa, 11 sulfur and 13 fresh turned charcoals, and mix them with a little water as to form a cake when rolled out on a board. This is dried on a clean sheet of paper placed in a warm situation, and afterwards crumbled into grains.

Early documents indicate that as early as 1805, a Neil McCoy was sent to Lexington, Kentucky to set up the manufacturing of gunpowder for the government. In 1810, Lexington had six-powder mill in operation.

One of the other components of gunpowder was sulfur in a 10% ratio. Sulfur appears to have been available to the early settlers by at least two sources. Iron Pyrite and mineral springs. Christopher Gist in his travels around Pilot Knob near Clay City, described in his journal an interesting item: "Here I found a place where the stones shined like high colored brass, the heat of the sun drew out of them a kind or borax only something sweeter; some of which I brought into the Ohio Company, though I believe it was nothing but a sort of sulfur."

What Mr. Gist found was Iron Pyrite or fool's gold, an iron sulfide, with high sulfur content. How the early settlers extracted the sulfur from the iron is not clear.
One way may have been in the application of heat.

There are several types of mineral springs where sulfur may have been obtained. The most common ones are Chalybeate, Sulfur and Alum. A Chalybeate spring is referenced as a corner between two tracts on Chimney Top in Wolfe County, and Swango Springs near Hazel Green was once a resort famous for the sulfur water.

It is not clear how large a gunpowder operation was in Powder Mill Branch nor the period of production. Little physical evidence remains and best guesses of the old timers place the mill on the left side of the creek just before the forks.

THE HUNTERS TRACT

This tract was once known as McGowan land. McGowan sold on February 23, 1867 to John Anderson and a group of wealthy Bluegrass businessmen a 5400-acre tract of land in the gorge. The purpose of this transaction was to provide this group a place for hunting and fishing trips. This included land along the Red River, around Fish trap, Duncan Branch, Gladie Creek, and Copperas Creek. The tract was finally bought by the Red River Lumber Company on January 11, 1911 and was called the Hunters Tract in this deed.

Red River was apparently well known at an early date. Dr. Thomas Walker crossed Red River in 1750 calling it the Big Creek. Christopher Gist explored along the Red in 1751 and proclaimed it "the roughest country I have ever seen."

It is a matter of record that in 1791 William Sudduth, a land surveyor came to the Red River in the employ of Eli Cleveland and John Morton. The records show that in 1791, Eli Cleveland and John Morton entered 1483 acres of land of two-treasury warrants No. 15.132 and 12.128 on a branch of Red River to include an old camp (John Swift?) in the center.

It appears, however, that Daniel Boone was more interested in Red River, since we find him returning repeatedly. In 1782, he entered two tracts of land in the records of Kentucky. One tract contained 1000 acres and the other 500 acres. Both tracts were on Red River.

Besides the privilege of flowing through the Red River Gorge, the river has seen its share of activity. From ancient man who established his villages along the riverbanks, to the early white settlers who farmed the river bottoms, the Red has been a river of opportunity.

THE BRANHAM PLACE

Along the bottoms of the Red River across from Parched Corn Creek is a hand hewn stone chimney with a four-foot mantle stone bearing the many cuts of tedious shaping. A cut rock foundation indicates a log house about 20 x12 feet. This was at the time the roadway was on the south side of the river.

It was here in this quiet valley that Wesley Branham lived out his life beside the Red, a river of conflicting emotions, most times peaceful, but sometimes a raging wall of water. Wesley farmed the narrow bottomland along the river, however no evidence remains. The area is now a thick canebrake, but the remains of the chimney are still visible from the present roadway. Pictured below are Wesley and Molly Branham.

NADA TUNNEL BITS

From the shadowy bore of Nada Tunnel come these stories.

James Spurlock worked on the west side (Nada) of the tunnel and was responsible for setting the blast to blow out the tunnel. According to folklore, he lit damp dynamite one morning and all they found of his body was his mustache hanging in a tree.

Floyd Brewer also worked on the tunnel and he recalls only two bad accidents that happened while construction was in progress. One man, Charles McNabb, was blown up while thawing dynamite and the other man, Will Ashley, got both legs cut off by a train.

A Mr. John Smith, of McCausey Ridge, was reputably the first person to crawl through the tunnel.

Old timers say the first few shots in the tunnel were put in wrong. Look on the Nada side and you can see the tunnel is crooked. Blasters say they followed where the engineer set the stakes. The engineer said the blasting was wrong. Whoever was right or wrong, the work continued on the tunnel, and the deviation is plainly visible today.

According to old timers, Orlando Rogers was the first man to drill the first row of shotholes for the dynamite on the east side of the tunnel.

On the east side of the tunnel on the right just as you exit, up a steep bank to a rock house, there was a large two-room building for the workers. One room was the kitchen and the other the dining room. "Uncle" Alex Grayson and his wife and daughters cooked for the crews. The lumber for the building was hauled by train to the west side of the tunnel. Than it was hoisted to the top of the cliff with rope and lowered to the ground on the east side.

Traveling through Nada Tunnel from west to east is a clearly visible rock formation that has been called the Great Stone Face. Some believe the rock bears a remarkable resemblance to one of the area's most famous pioneer explorers -- Daniel Boone. The next time you pass through the tunnel, observe this stone configuration and judge for yourself.

Dillard Smith helped put the first shot into the tunnel by drilling three holes and putting in three shots, when they were "rolling the heading." (The initial horizontal passage for a tunnel). Smith indicated that sandstone was harder to pull than limestone which would break easily. When you shoot limestone, it will just bust up and pull out. In the sandstone it was one pull, six feet at a time. According to Smith the dog that was killed in the explosion of dynamite (Tragedy at Nada Tunnel) was a big shepherd dog.

Building the tunnel (13' x 12' x 900' long) through the sandstone created dangers such as shifting ground pressure, water and gases which could cause an explosion. The top part of the tunnel came out first, followed by the bench. The refuse was hauled in carts with horses and mules as it was shot out and dumped.

GRAVE OF FLEM KING

On a lonely hemlock, shrouded bench just across Indian Creek from the old swimming hole is the lone grave of a man who logged this area and supposedly died of smallpox. He was a logger for Broadhead-Garrett Lumber Company. The gravestone inscription is F. King. I have been told his name was Fleming King and another old timer remembered him as Offenal King. He was allegedly buried in this lone grave because of the fear of smallpox. He was born in Franklin County, VA in 1814 and died around 1880 on Indian Creek in Menifee County, Kentucky. He was the son of Moses King.

Mrs. King ran a boarding house at Edwards Branch in the early 1900's. Later, they moved off and just left the one in Edwards Branch and built a new boarding house at Orchard Branch on Indian Creek. The Broadhead –Garret Lumber Company brought in the lumber to build the house because Mrs. King was keeping the loggers. It was located on the upper end of the bottom between the road and creek. The building was a long, with a kitchen and place to eat with enough room to keep 8-10 men. Mrs. King bought vegetables from Mrs. Henry Skidmore. What happened to Mrs. King, I was unable to determine.

159

MOVING THE KLABER HOUSE

The Klaber house was a large imposing log structure for the time.   Built around 1894, it was a big house with four rooms, a dogtrot, and three attic rooms. Bill Profitt described the place as having many outbuildings, including a barn, a corn crib, an outhouse and smokehouse.

In the late 1930's Floyd Byrd obtained possession of the house and moved it log by log to Rose Orchard on Red River. Jasper Spencer reassembled the house. Byrd bought new windows, material for the roof and other supplies. Before he could complete the work, the house burned of an unknown cause.

Part of the house while at Klaber Branch is visible in the picture below. Stella Tackett Ledford in front of the house was the mother of the famous Lily Mae
Ledford.

A SHOOTING AT GLADIE CREEK

If you should visit Gladie Creek Historic Site and wander across the road, you may happen upon the remains of on old cabin that was once the scene of a killing and another man wounded.
Three men got into an argument over unknown subject matter. The exact reason is lost to history, but it was in this cabin that Clayton
McKenzie shot and killed Lester King and wounded Verlen Martin.

It is said that Clayton McKenzie was later killed by lightning while under a cliff near the cabin taking shelter from a thunderstorm. Another version of the story is that Clayton received a 21-year sentence, served 6 and died in Morgan County.

Other occupants of the cabin included Stanley and Nellie Gibbs, Billy and Golden Gibbs, and a Branham. The old cabin while still standing is pictured below. The young lad is unknown.

GORGE COAL MINING

Some small-scale coal mining has occurred in the gorge area; however, coal resources have not been consistent enough to encourage large-scale commercial mining. Powell Rose, a Chimney Rock resident, mined coal in the area about 1850. He loaded the coal in White Oak barges, which he constructed, and floated to Frankfort where he disposed of the entire load including the barge.

The coal was described on Wolfpen and Chimney Rock as being a seam 23 to 25 inches thick.

A coalmine was opened near the cemetery at Gladie in 1946. Jim Ward and Vernie Brewer of Pomeroyton paid Stanley Gibbs $1.25 per ton for the coal. They sold it in and around Pomeroyton. The mine was around 100 feet deep with a 12-14 inch thick seam. It was good coal with low sulfur.

A good seam of cannel coal exits on Parched Corn Creek over 36 inches thick in places.

Arch Carpenter drilled the gas well near the sorghum mill in 1937. The well was about 1200 feet deep and mostly shale gas which does not blow out tools. Another well was drilled across Gladie (west) where the new bridge is located. Fill now covers well. Gas from the first well was piped to the Gladie house. The well was plugged in 1996.

SWIFTSVILLE

An act to establish the county of Wolfe in 1860 under the Laws of Kentucky directs the seat of justice for Wolfe County shall be, and the same is, located at or near Swiftsville (now Morgan county), at a point agreed upon by the commissioners hereinafter appointed, and the name of said seat of justice shall be Campton. Dr. Clark of Powell county, S. R. Turner of Morgan County, William Day, of Breathitt County, and Major Hampton, of Owsley County, and Thos. Sewell, of Breathitt, a majority of whom may act, are hereby appointed commissioners to locate the seat of justice.

The name Swiftsville is shrouded in obscurity. Apparently it was named for John Swift of silver mine fame who was supposed to have explored this area during the years 1760-1769. Campton (for Camp town) was also named after John Swift, as well as the creek meandering through the settlement.

During the years mentioned above, Swift carried in supplies and took out silver bars and minted coins. Beleaguered by Indians, recalcitrance of his workers, and various other problems, Swift is reputed to have walled up his mine and headed for England to seek support for his venture. He did not return until fifteen years later, having supposedly been imprisoned. By this time he had become blind from a sickness and was never able to find his mine even though he had marked it with various symbols.

The name Swiftsville must have endured for many years since it was not renamed Campton until 1860. Swiftsville may have simply suffered the same fate as Beaver Pond and received a new name when it became a county seat. Both exist now only in the footnotes of history.

"LONG GEORGE" SPENCER

According to local folklore about the time the Mountain Central Railroad was built, Long George established a store around Glencairn, and somehow obtained a copy of Swift's Journal. His version of the journal stated that near the Turtleback Rock there were three white oak trees growing from a common stump. Long George is reputed to have located this marker along with the grave of Swift's former partner, J. C. Blackburn, and above it a stone bearing the date 1825. Since Blackburn had died previous to 1800, there is no logical reasoning for this except the date was read erroneously.

Long George claims to have discovered the long lost Swift's silver mine but never recovered the silver. He tried twice, but "strange things happened." Once, while digging in a pit, a rock fell on him. Later, a girl dressed in white appeared at the entrance to his shaft and told him, "Get out and quit looking for silver."

He did as he was told and remarked ever after that he would die with the secret, quoting Haggai, the prophet who said, "The silver is mine, and the gold is mine, saith the Lord of hosts." With these words on his lips, Long George Spencer of Glencairn died with his secret.

CHAIR CRAFTSMAN IN THE GORGE

Using a shaving horse similar to the one on display at the Gladie Creek Historic Site, many old-timers fabricated their own chairs from saplings. Suitable woods included oak, maple and ash for the post and back. The seat was made by weaving splits of white oak, or strips of hickory or poplar bark. Cane and plaited corn shucks were also used. The standard weave for the seat was the herringbone pattern, a series of over and under lapping the bark or splits. The bark for the seats was stripped from the trees in the spring while the sap was up making the separation of the bark from the tree easy. The stripping was started near the butt of the tree in sections about two inches wide and continued upwards as long as possible or until the preferred length was obtained. Poplar stripped the easiest, but was less durable. White oak splits were traditionally used in this area for bottoming chairs and basket making. Splits were made using the froe and splitting horse to convert the original white oak sapling (four to six inches in diameter) into eights. The actual making of the splits now begins. Starting at the butt end of one of the eights, it was split in half and split again continuing in this manner until the splits were of the desired thickness.

The above photo shows a small finished chair consisting of two long post, two short posts, eight short rounds and two back pieces. The bottom is cane.

THE H.C. FARMER HOUSE

Seldon Skidmore, who eventually demolished the old Farmer house in order to make room for a new brick residence about 1978, last occupied the old residence. The new house was built on the same location as the old one. The original house was a wooden two-story structure built about 1875 by Hezekiah Bowen, later sold to Henry Carter Farmer who came to the Red River near Indian Creek from Harlan County, Kentucky in 1884. The photo below circa 1890's captures in the back row Carter and Isom Farmer. In the front row pictured left to right are Abner Farmer, H.C. Farmer (seated) and six children with Rachel Farmer on extreme right (with broom). The names of the younger ones are unknown at this time, except for Oliver, Cordia and Daniel not identified.

Pictured below is a full view of the H.C. Farmer house showing
two stories and log outbuilding. The area was formerly known
as Haystack, Kentucky. A post office (Haystack) was established

173

on August 13, 1888 just across the road from the residence. The Haystack post office was discontinued on March 5, 1913 and the mail moved to Fagan Post Office. H.C. Farmer sold the house and many acres of land to Henry Skidmore in 1910. His son, Seldon Skidmore, was born here and was in continuous residence until he built the new brick house in 1978.

FRED KLABER

Fred Klaber was born on Klaber Branch off Gladie Creek on February 4, 1894, son of Jacob and Julia Klaber. He logged the Red River for many years. Pictured below is a logging camp on Red River. Fred is first in line on horseback.

Logging the Red River.

Fred Klaber is astride the donkey. He died in Franklin, Ohio on October 21, 1970.

A LOG RAFTING PRIMER

Log rafting on the Red River was a slow clumsy thing to manage. Rigging was a rope or a length of grapevine. Once a raft was adrift and caught in the flood tide, its fate was more nearly in the river's control than in that of the crew. Rafts that floated the Red River were assembled so that the logs ran abreast of the current riding low in the water to take advantage of the driving force of the tide. On the larger rivers, the logs were lashed endwise to the current. Poplar, chestnut, basswood and occasionally pine were used as floaters. To give the raft maximum flotation denser oak, hickory, walnut, ash and maple logs were placed between the floaters. When all the logs were in place, split oak or hickory binders were pegged across the outer ends. In early days, auger holes were bored into which hardwood pegs were driven through the binders to hold the raft together. "Chain Dogs" replaced this method in later years. (See Log Rafting the Red River)

The logging companies (and individual loggers) produced branding irons with the owners selected symbol or mark. These brands were registered at the local courthouse. These brands were stamped on the log to identify the owner. There were many timber thieves who corralled runaway logs, branded or unbranded. They were

177

supposed to return the branded logs to their owners or drift them into mill booms were buyers give the rightful owners credit. Oftentimes the thieves "dehorned" branded logs by sawing off the ends and stamping their own brand on the freshly cut surface. (See Log Brands of the Red River)

The men who undertook this dangerous way of life were in many cases farmers who sought cash income by engaging in logging as a part time occupation between farming seasons. Men and boys sawed logs and hauled them to creek banks or cliff-top log dumps to ready for rafting at the first tide. There were also classes of men hired by the logging companies known as river men (See River men) whose job was to manage the log rafts and free log jambs.

The early river men who ran the Red and Kentucky River system were bound for Frankfort a distance of over 200 miles. Once the log raft had been scaled and paid, the rafting crew began the long trip home. In the early years log prices ranged from $2.50 to $5.00 per thousand feet. A good medium –sized log raft at Frankfort in 1890 yielded between $150 and $300.

RUSH BRANCH STEAM MILL

On October 4, 1899 Wythe and Sidney Chester, the firm of Chester Bros, being indebted to J. T. Day in the amount of $684.75 mortgaged certain personal property located on Rush Branch in Powell County to secure the payment:

One complete steam mill and saw works, engine (25 hp) made by Lowe and Bodley. In addition, six single flanged tramcars complete. The property was warranted free from encumbrances with the exception due L.H. Fauguar.

This was the same Chester as the firm of Horton & Chester that logged Wolfpen Creek in 1905.

The old engine is still visible at the mouth of Rush Branch.

THE UNFATHOMABLE DATE

In a remote rockshelter near Sky Bridge Road, which once was the scene of a Saltpeter operation is a mysterious date carved on a boulder. The date is inscribed as March 27, 1712 with the initials JFB immediately underneath. If this date is authentic, it precedes Daniel Boone by some 57 years and John Swift by 48 years.

Some Archeologists believe the date may be as old as the carving indicates. Since niter mining in this area was mostly during the war of 1812 or the War Between the States, this date precedes even these periods. Kentucky became a State in 1789. Before that, the Gorge area was part of Virginia called Kentucky County. This makes the initials of JBF difficult to locate on land grants or census records. We may never know the name of the initials inscribed by someone at some date in this long abandoned saltpeter works.

The date and unknown initials will probably become just a footnote in history. All efforts to identify this seemingly authentic carving on a rock have been futile. Perhaps one of the future readers will unveil the mystery.

A TINCTURE OF LIGHTFOOT

Interviews with old timers revealed there once was a time in the Red River Gorge when you could not walk into a hollow without finding a moonshine still. One location still bears the name Moonshiners Arch for the operation that was carried out in its shelter.

Moonshine, or illicit whiskey, was a main source of income for many families trying to get by during the prohibition years. A restored still at Gladie Historic site is near the location of the original moonshine still as pointed out by the operator to the author many years ago. This old-timer helped set up the still in the same manner as it was in former times. This still, of course, is not operational, but could be if the concrete was removed from inside the cooker or pot.

182

The name moonshine was derived from the clandestine operations and the "kick" to the liquid. The product was also called corn squeezing, white lightening, corn, and tincture of light foot, ruckus juice and other names. At one time in the gorge area, there were several types of sills in operation. The simplest and probably the best is briefly described below as told to me by one of the old-time operators:

First find a location for the still where it can be hidden and smoke from the cooker concealed or dispersed. The location must be near water or have some means of bringing water to the site. Next, construct the furnace and flue from native stone and chink with clay. Use copper sheets to fabricate the cooker and cap, bottom and top halves of the sill. Everything must fit or the still would leak. Bend copper (3/4 to one inch) tubing by coiling it around a stump, then slipping it off, to fabricate the worm. Copper was used because the beer would not stick to it.

 The process of moonshine begins in the cooker where water and corn meal are mixed together and heated by the furnace fire. It is left to boil about thirty-five to forty minutes then drained into a nearby barrel. This is done as many times as there are waiting barrels. Once the mixture is put in barrels more corn meal is stirred in to let the hot contents cook it alone. It is then let sit until the next day. Next the mixture is thinned and malt added to barrel. Rye is also added to get the mixture working and produce a cap. The barrels are covered and let sit overnight.

The new mixture should be working by now and it is called beer at this point. Once more, the mixture is left to work overnight and mixed again the next day and left for two more days. By the fifth day, the mixture should be ready to run. At this point beer is added to the cooker, and some is added to the thumper keg where the copper tubing is coiled. The beer is stirred into the cooker, sealed and left to work on its own. The steam will hit the cool temperature in the thumping keg and began "thumping." Soon after the thumping stops the whiskey starts and is caught in jars or other suitable containers after going through a funnel lined with cloth and hickory coals to remove impurities.

An old still in the Red River Gorge. Note enclosed wooden barrels.

According to old-timers, the best wood to fuel the furnace was ash, which produces a steady heat and gives off little smoke. Hickory and oak were also used. Smoke was usually a problem only at the beginning of a run.

When the fire gets going, it gives off heat waves rather than smoke. This is why old-time moon shiners started their fires just before dawn, so that by daylight the smoke was diffused enough to escape detection. This still was destroyed by Federal Agents or Revenuers, as they were known at the time. Note the metal drums and wooden thumping keg. Many such remains may be seen in the area today as a last vestige of one of the most fascinating Red River Gorge endeavors.

GRAFFITI – SOCIAL PROBLEM OR TREASURE?

Petroglyphs (prehistoric rock carving) and Pictographs (prehistoric rock painting) are now considered national treasures and are protected under law. This ancient scrabble of early man's inscriptions is perhaps the earliest form of a written language.

These Rock-Writers wanted their scribings to endure, seemingly, cutting the groves of their carvings sometimes an inch or deeper into the rock surface. Than, went to the additional chore of rubbing the grooves smooth. In Genesis 11, 1, there is a passage which reads: "And the whole earth was of one language, and of one speech". Petroglyphs are in every quarter of the earth, and perhaps this may serve as a testimony that a written language was understood over the entire world.

The modern day rock carver appears to be reaching out with an unconscious wish for immortality as names and initials are cut into conspicuous places. Except in a few cases, there appears to be no systematic reason for this practice, while in the case of the ancients the carvings appear to be for the guidance, attainment and safety of others who followed. These ancient carvings are not considered graffiti, but a valuable part of our heritage, while modern day carvings have captured this title, and are considered acts of vandalism. Some historic cravings seem to relate events or happenings in the lives of the early settlers. The following historic carvings relate an event that must have strongly impressed the carver: The story appears to be an early settler died in a remote drainage of the Red River Gorge. The body was placed in wagon hitched to two horses for the journey to his final resting place. On the route was a steep cliff barely negotiable by the horses and wagon. The deceased's sons, who owned the horses, began to argue over which horse could pull the most loads. During the course of this discussion, as they were on the steep cliff, the coffin slipped from the wagon and pounded over the edge. One son became so angry he shot and killed the other. In the days that followed, his remorse became consequently immense, moving him to carve the story in stone at the cliff edge. The story is depicted in rock by these symbols:

The watch represents the time of day, the Stevens the weapon used, and the hand depicts the arm of the law. The date is obscure, but this happened in the 1930's.

What is graffiti? Webster's definition reads: "To scratch, scribble. A style of writing, inscriptions and drawings found on rocks or on the walls of ancient ruins."

This is far removed from the wall scrawl of modern graffitist whom appears to aimlessly and randomly spread their oftentimes-inane message of doubtful value.

The graffiti that may be considered vandalism today could be tomorrow's treasure.

There is a great concern the record of 30,000 years of life in America is being destroyed by artifact hunters who are plundering our heritage. Might today's graffiti be part of that heritage at some distant time? Conversely, there are those who believe that ancient inscriptions are mere doodling, and if they had any meaning at all, it perished with the individual who carved them. In the Red River Gorge, the similarity of tracks, circles and other symbols distantly removed from each other would indicate these carvings were much more than just an aimless scribble to help pass the long winter months or periods of idleness in the rock shelters.

Archaeologists are now engaged in the study of humankind's history – especially the 30,000 years of life in America. Is it possible that today's wall scrawl will be the focus of some future study? An unfolding Rosetta stone? The possibility is remote, of course, but the theory does create an interesting thought for those who deface some of our natural wonders. It might well generate a justification for the previously mentioned action, at least in objective, in the hope they will be remembered for time immortal.

The inscribed faces of thousands of Red River Gorge rocks, and their kindred over the earth, have endured and survived the tortures of millenniums, silent in forbearance, waiting for someone to decipher their message and in gratitude travel onward/upward toward their destiny.

In addition, what a cause for gratitude! It may have been learned of how and when these inscriptions came to be distributed "all over the earth", by a seemingly suddenly dislodged and destitute people – "Of one language."

Such knits well with Holy Writ (Genesis 11, 1-9). An in the presence of such truth, in my humble insignificance, I can only testify; "It is written"-On stone.

PINE RIDGE FOREST CAMP

According to an article in the August 18, 1938 issue more then 4000 visitors have registered at the Pine Ridge Forest Camp in Wolfe County since January 1.
This announcement was made at the Cumberland National Forest Supervisor's office in Winchester.

The forest camp, located at the site of the Pine Ridge fire tower was designed to accommodate campers, picnickers, hikers and tourist. Drinking water, fire places, tables benches, sanitary facilities and picnic shelter are conveniently located.

The largest number to resister was on July 4, 1938 when 274 persons recorded their visit in the registry book.

Picnic shelter at Pine Ridge

RED RIVER BRIDGE

In 1938 construction of a new bridge over the Red River at the Wolfe/Menifee County line, was started to replace the old wooden bridge. The new bridge was built on masonry abutments and piers consisting of two 65 foot spans and one 120 span. Steel delivery to the site was by truck, over the Red River Road. (Now 715) The task of building the bridge was assigned to Pine Ridge Veterans camp F-9.

Wooden Bridge across Red River prior to 1938

**New bridge construction across Red River just downstream
from old wood bridge**

THE CLAY CITY TIMES, OCTOBER 2,1937

Members of the Winchester Lions Club will visit the Cumberland National Forest on Sunday. The tour will be conducted by members of the Forest Supervisor's Staff and the Red River District Ranger.

The group will leave Winchester at 9:30 A.M. and drive east to the CCC Veterans Camp F-9 near Stanton. An inspection of the camp will be made and dinner served.

Leaving the CCC camp, the group will proceed to the Pine Ridge Fire Tower, Sky Bridge, Lions Club Boy's Camp site and through Red River Gorge to Frenchburg.

Veterans Camp F-9 at Bowen, Kentucky

FIFTH ANNIVERSARY OF CCC

From the March 31, 1938 issue comes the following story of the fifth anniversary of the CCC to be observed at Stanton, Kentucky on April 5th.

In commemoration of the 5th anniversary of the CCC an open house and program will be held in Camp F-9, Company 1559, CCC Vets, Stanton (Bowen), Kentucky, on April 5, 1938. The public is invited to attend this program and to inspect the Camp and Work Projects. The events for the day are as follows:

1:00 to 2:30 P.M. –Reception of visitors and inspection of camp.
2:30 P.M.—Address by Mr. A. H. Anderson, Asst. Supervisor, Cumberland
        National Forest.
        Explanation of the Work Projects by Mr. C.D. Juett, Camp
        Superintendent.
        Unveiling of monument and dedicatory exercises.
        Lt. Richard Hoyer, Camp Commander will welcome visitors and
        introduce speakers.
3:30 to 5:00 P.M. –Inspection of the Work Project. Trucks will be available to take
        who care to go to the scene of the work now being carried on by Camp
        members.
6:30 P.M. –Motion picture show.

CCC Camp F-9 Company 1559 V at Bowen, Kentucky

SALT MAKING

If you look at a topographic map of the Red River Gorge, you may note Salt Fork of Gladie Creek. Since creeks are usually named after someone who lived there or some activity which took place, it is logical to assume that the area was the scene of early salt making, especially after the discovery of several pieces of iron kettle at one of the licks on this fork.

The brine from these sources appearing at the surface as springs, the basins of which rich in salt, were formerly the gathering place for wild game and were known as "licks." Salt was used in large quantities at this time for the preservation of meat.

To obtain the salt the early settler hung an ordinary pot or kettle over an open fire
and filled it with brine water from the spring. This was boiled for some time in the kettles and the salt obtained by evaporation, leaving a thin residue of salt in the kettle. The labor of salt making was prodigious. It took 840 gallons of a weak brine to yield a single bushel of salt, although very fine springs were reputed to give a bushel for every eighty gallons. A bushel of salt in Daniel Boone's time was worth
about $1.25.

There were many salt springs or licks in Kentucky, and even before the early pioneers, making salt was a major extractive industry for the Indians using large clay vessels.

Salt making was not merely laborious it was also dangerous. The Indians knew where the salt licks were located and salt-making parties, like Boone's, had to go out in force ready to defend themselves at any time. This activity was apparently carried out in the fall or winter months and, depending on the strength of the brine water, may have occupied several days or weeks. The early pioneer usually considered winter as the best time for salt making, since it was warm work and the Indians usually stayed close to their villages during bitter weather.

According to records of the pioneer settlement at Boonesborough, the salt making "continued for some weeks, and several horse-loads of salt had been sent back to the station."

THREATENED AND ENDANGERED SPECIES OF THE RED RIVER GORGE

Oftentimes you hear about an animal or plant called a T&E, a species threatened with extinction. Have you ever been curious about such animals or plants? Would it make a difference to you if a particular species of animal or plant lives or disappears forever from the Red River Gorge?

How does a species become endangered? If your first impulse is to say hunting, think it over. In fact, the majority of animals, fish, birds and reptiles on the T&E list are in trouble because they are small, inconspicuous, unnoticed and virtually ignored species. They are threatened and endangered due to lack of knowledge about them. Because humankind is concerned about species, which are hunted, they have been studied, protected and managed for years. Careful watch has been kept over the habitat and number of species. Their movements have been closely tabulated, and the harvest by sportsman controlled to insure the continuation of optimum population levels. If the population of a species declines, quail for example, or if a fish kill, occurs on a lake or river, people notice and take action. However, in the same area, there may be a species of salamander or goldenrod, which has evolved in response to specific conditions of a rather specialized habitat. When this habitat is impacted by human activities, the salamander or goldenrod environment may be changed so drastically they are doomed to extinction. The Red Cockaded Woodpecker nest only in old pines, the very trees many people cut down.

Another problem faced by many of these T&E species it that when the average person does take notice, they are likely to be less than kindly disposed toward these species. Checking the Red River Gorge T&E list we find species of rats, bats, skunks, mice, and so forth. This is hardly a list of one's best-loved wildlife. Some of the listed species are birds of prey, too often mistakenly accused of killing chickens and depleting populations of songbirds. Add snakes, turtles, salamanders, tree frogs, and we have a representative of almost all of the creeping, crawling, slithering, scurrying denizens that invoke a negative reaction in many humans.

In fact, by this time you may be asking yourself, why bother? Indeed, why should we be concerned about the fate of the Big-Eared Bat or the three-toed salamander? First, we can appeal to our own self-interest. We do not know that many of these species may prove to be beneficial in ways not yet discovered. We should also remember that each species is unique in itself. Destroy any species and you destroy a historical record older by far than any works of man. We should develop a respect for the rights of other inhabitants of the land. This does not imply we should no longer hunt and fish. Often, as in the case of overpopulated deer herds, controlled hunting and harvest is one way of insuring the survival of the species. What we do need is a reversal of the reckless killing attitude and habitat destruction in the name of progress. While we cannot permit the wholesale destruction of crops by insects, we should not excuse the indiscriminate application of pesticides, which also kill beneficial birds, insects and animals.

What can we do to help these species? In many cases the Threatened and Endangered Species Act is only a partial solution. It is doubtful if a person killing a three-toed salamander or using a snail darter for bait would be convicted of a crime.

Finally, we need to remember there are T&E species. Do not kill a snake or bat simply because they are in the same locale as you are. Our national emblem, the Bald Eagle, was one of the many species of wildlife in danger of becoming extinct. Most of the other T&E species are not as well known as this bird, but all are historical monuments. It would be a dubious honor indeed to go down in history as the person who destroyed the last Bald Eagle.

A study of ancient history reveals that 19 of 21 civilizations perished from the face of the earth because of an inability to learn an existence cannot be maintained without the conservation of all our natural resources. If we cannot learn this lesson, than man indeed may become the endangered species.

SUGAR TREE BOTTOM

The Slusher house was located south of the Red River across from the junction on Kentucky 77 & 715 in an area locally known as Sugar Tree Bottoms. The house was a small wood frame situated on a prominent knoll overlooking the Red River. Jarve and Alice Slusher raised their family here, 2 sons and 3 daughters. Alice died in 1935 and Jarve in 1942. All traces of the house, except for a few loose rock, are gone now, a victim of time and weathering.

The Broadhead-Garrett Lumber Company had a narrow gauge railroad running through Sugar Tree Bottom and in a conveyance from Broadhead to J.B Finch of some 2, 235 acres in 1919 there was reserved a logging railroad and equipment along with the right to remove the said railroad and equipment. Remnants of the railroad, except for the grade, have vanished.

A historic trail , aptly named the Broadhead-Garret Trail, is possible on the south side of the Red River along the old railroad grade, from KY 77 Bridge (link with Martins Fork) to the swinging Bridge near Rose Orchard and Chimney Top Creek.(link with the Sheltowee Trace). Along the route (near Rush Branch) are the rusted remains of an old engine from the logging days.

HANG GLIDING IN THE GORGE

Workers at Raven Rock were busily installing a hang-gliding ramp at the top of the rock in preparation for the 1976 Labor Day Weekend. Before this weekend passed into history, two Cincinnati hang-gliders were killed and a third suffered a broken foot.

Raven Rock, a 600 foot promontory in the lower gorge, appeared to the private landowner to be ideal location for hang-gliding, especially since he had been contacted by a group from Cincinnati about the possibility of holding a gliding competition there. On the east side of the rock, the owner constructed a large wooden ramp hanging out over the top of the cliff. The hang-gliders would have a good landing zone in the cleared area below.

September 6, 1976 dawned to a host of hang-glider pilots assembling at the top of Raven Rock for the initial such competition in the Red River Gorge. When the first hang-glider plummeted to his death, pilot error was blamed and a somber mood overcame the crowd, but the meet continued. After the second hang-glider was killed and a third injured, wind currents and faulty equipment were answerable.
One glider pilot remarked that Raven Rock was too dangerous for the sport. The competition was cancelled, and the on lookers dispersed.

Normally, the gorge is not thought of as a place of death and tragedy, but rather as a situate for the celebration of life. 1976 marked the first and last hang-gliding at Raven Rock. Today the rock is used primarily as an observation point and for rock climbing, with a route morbidly named Black Death.

SLADE GUARD STATION

The Slade Guard Station was constructed in 1935 at a cost of $8740.00 at Slade to provide a dwelling for the District Assistant of the newly formed Red River Ranger District of the future Cumberland National Forest. The house measured about 32x 30 feet and was a two-story building. The ground floor contained a kitchen, bath, bedroom, living room and office. The upper floor contained two bedrooms.

Occupants of the house were U.S. Forest Service employees, with Joe Mulk being the first, the second Wilbur Rose and the last Clarence Henson. A shop building was constructed the same year, 84 x32 feet at a cost of $5000.

Around 1968 the building was part of an exchange with the State of Kentucky for parcels along the Mountain Parkway.

THE SHADOW OF TIME

In the early 1960s, there developed a "return to nature" concept and the Red River Gorge began to be visited in overwhelming numbers. Thus began a series of ironic and paradoxical events, which were designed to "save" the gorge, but in effect has hastened the area's demise.

In 1962 the Army Corps of Engineers announced plans to build a flood control dam on the Red River. That same year, the Sierra Club lodged a formal project against the dam. The next six years brought a flood of protests against the dam from other conservation groups, academic organizations, and literally hundreds of self-proclaimed gorge "experts" all voicing their avowed convictions that the gorge must be saved from the dam. This drew the attention of a new horde of visitors and by the end of the decade; the gorge was being flooded with people, not water. These people swarmed all over the gorge to see the place where the Corps of Engineers was proposing to flood with water, and in doing so, they succeeded in destroying much of it themselves. They came with soft drink and beer cans and tons of paper, and when they had departed, the trash was left behind.

Then in November 1967, Supreme Court Justice William O. Douglas made his famous hike up the Red River, attracting nearly 600 people. Apparently, no thought was given to the environmental effects of a crowd of nearly 600 tramping their way through the flora and fauna.

In March 1969, Governor Louie Nunn asked the crops to consider an alternate location downstream. Kentucky Senator John Cooper boosted Nunn's announcement of an alternate site. The Corps agreed to consider the alternate site, located about five miles downstream from the original location. Early in 1971, the COE announced the lower site, but some feared the new location would in many ways be more damaging to the environment than the original proposal.

Meanwhile, two groups were forming. On July 5, 1973, a group of Powell County residents organized Save Our Red River (SORR) with the purpose of opposing the construction of the Red River Dam. The Red River Gorge Legal Defense Fund, Inc. was organized on July 2, 1974 by a coalition of Powell County citizens and national\ local environmental and conservation groups as a means for legal action in connection with the proposed construction of the Red River Dam.

By September 11, 1975, the controversy was still raging and on this date, Governor Julian Carroll announced his opposition to the Dam project. The Army Corps of Engineers in turn recommended to Congress that the Red River Dam not be constructed due to the opposition of the Governor. Subsequently, the project was shelved for the time, but could be reauthorized.

Environmentalists wanted a full hearing on the project instead of a dismissal. They hoped the hearing would lead to a permanent court order to block the dam. Eighteen years later, their hopes were finally realized when in 1993, a section of the Red River was proclaimed a National Wild and Scenic River, the first for Kentucky.

The National Wild and Scenic River flows within the silhouette of Sky Bridge, an arch that has kept a mythical watch of changes to the area over these many years. (See Saga of an Arch).

This designation has finally chased away the shadow of the Red River Dam, and will protect the river in its natural state for future generations.

In the words of Gifford Pinchot: "Conservation of natural resources is the key to the safety and prosperity of the American people and all of the people of the world for all time to come."

THE LONGEST WALK

On Saturday, November 18, 1967, a large crowd had gathered at the Wolfe/Menifee County line concrete bridge awaiting the arrival of U.S. Supreme Court Justice William O. Douglas. The Justice had agreed to lead a hike up Red River to Clifty Creek (about 1 ½ miles) to protest the proposed impoundment on the river. The restless group (about 600-800 strong) milled about peacefully.

Finally, about 1330 hours the Justice arrived along with his wife, addressed the group, and commenced to lead the hike upriver. The Kentucky Chapter of the Sierra Club promoted this hike. At one point, the Sierra Club counted 524 hikers along the trail. The protest was a partial success, but in a way, it may only have intensified the threat from man. It brought a colossal increase in visitation to the area, reaching a peak in 1972 of over one million visitors quintupling the visitation prior to 1967.

It has been 34 years since Justice Douglas made his famous walk up the Red River in protest of the proposed dam. The intervening years have wrought many changes since that long ago November day and the walk has continued in phantom footsteps these many years, readily apparent in defacement and destruction of various cultural resources. The petroglyph at Trinity was destroyed a few years ago by building a campfire squarely on top of it. This was perhaps the most significant rock art in the Red River Gorge. Forever silent now, with no prospect of deciphering the message. Increased littering, soil compaction, destruction of resources may be cited as typical of the problems associated with the present visitor overload.

For a time the area was called the site of the Justice Douglas hike, later abbreviated to Douglas Trail, an unofficial name that endures to this day.

THE FLOYD LEDFORD HOUSE

Floyd was the son of Joe Ledford. His twin brother, Charles, died an infant. In his later years, Floyd built a house, where the Sheltowee Trace Trailhead off Highway 715 is now located, about 1960. The residence was one story wood frame (705 sq ft) construction. He occupied this house until 1975 when ill health forced his move to Stanton. Used as a storage area for a period, it was remodeled in 1979 by Danny Morrison , who used the house for a weekend habitat. It was a great pleasure to stop by this house. Floyd was a great historian who could keep you spellbound with his reminisces for hours. He was a great "Teller of Tales".

The Floyd Ledford house is in the background. The swinging footbridge spans Red River and is the handiwork of Chester Morrison vintage 1964. The house is gone now, the last trace buried by a parking lot. Through it all the Red River has flowed serenely, and sometimes raging, keeping its powerful secrets.

THE INDIAN STAIRWAY

The well-known Indian Stairway is a series of about 50 indentations cut in the sheer face of a cliff to facilitate getting up or down. Although the popular belief is that ancient man cut the stairway, erosion tells a different story. The steps have scoured rapidly over the past 40 years eroding the niches so that there is little room to place the toe of a shoe. It does not appear, that as exposed to the elements as this feature, the erosion is slow. The stairway has a southern aspect. If you climb about halfway up the stairway and reach out your right hand full length of the arm, you will find an interesting dim outline of what appears to be a bird with no visible wings, two feet and a semblance of tail feathers. When this carving was found about 1971, it was covered with lichens. Removal of the lichens revealed a carving, which was incised to a depth of about one quarter inch, and did not approximate prehistoric.

Currently, after a long exposure to the weather, without the
        protection of the lichens
the carving is difficult to see. This in the space of some 30 years of weathering!

Another interesting supposition is niter miners to get to the ridge above cut the steps. There are the remains of a large niter mine at the head of Sargent's Branch just east of the stairway.

Whatever scenario is correct the Indian Stairway is fast losing its integrity as a prehistoric or historic site by the sheer volume of visitor use.

Note the carving on the right, just above the scale. The indentations on the left are the famed Indian Stairway.

GEORGE WASHINGTON PITTS

From the shadowy depths of Spaas Creek come these stories of
G.W. Pitts. They were told this way to me:

G.W. Pitts hailed from Beech River, Tennessee when he
migrated to Floyd County. Then on to Petre Trace arriving in
Spaas Creek in 1854. He took up land of the John Bradshaw
Patent of 50 acres, swapping his knife and gun for it. He also
bought an additional 500 acres of vacant land in 1854 at 5 cents
per acre.

It is reputed he fought and killed a wildcat with his knife on Bee
Branch of Spaas Creek. The wildcat ripped open his stomach of
G.W. before he succumbed to the knife wounds. Pitts held his
entrails in his hands and walked home, where he was sewed up
with linden thread and eventually recovered.

G.W. Pitts and Thomas Day were hunting wild hogs in little
Cordual Branch when a wild hog put up a vicious fight with the
dogs. Thomas Day thought he had climbed a tree and asked for
a light to see how to get down. The tree was a tall slim poplar on
the edge of the cliff and he was sitting on the ledge of cliff his
arms and legs wrapped around the tree and his feet hanging
over the cliff.

G.W. Pitts around 1891 had 99 stands of bees. He would sell
honey by the barrel, hauling it in a cart to Montgomery County.
He knew of a hive of bees in the cliff, and had always wanted an
even 100 stands, but never achieved his goal.

During the War between the States, G.W. Pitts hid his horses at
a rock house in Big Deer Park, about 300 feet from mouth of
Camp Branch, formerly called Bolez Branch. He had at least
one iron gray mare taken by the southern army.

The 1870 Census list G.W. Pitts as 54 years old and a farmer, his wife Sarah, four daughters, Emma, Clemie, Sarah Alice and Nancy Ellen.   Three sons, John, Jona and Alford.

Somewhere around 1900, a few years before his death, G.W. Pitts was riding his horse just above the mouth of Cold spring Fork of Bear Branch off Spaas Creek when the horse fell over the hill with him. He held it by the bridle until men logging in Bear Branch came to his rescue.

George Washington Pitts (1817-1907) was buried on Spaas Creek at the mouth of Bee Branch, near where he wrestled and killed the wildcat.

LOGGING

When settlers first came to the Red River Gorge, there was an abundance of virgin timber. A luxuriant forest of hardwoods mixed with conifers blanketed Red River and its tributaries when pioneers explored the area at a very early date. The journal of Dr. Thomas Walker in 1750 marveled at the significant trees of mammoth proportions.

Timber cutting has been practiced since these early days on a small scale until about 1890. Trees had been laboriously hewn with axes, split with wedges, ripped with man-powered whipsaws or sawed the water –powered mills. Logs were cut with crosscut saws and hauled by oxen or mules to the nearest stream or river to be floated downstream to the mills. Logging crews had to wait for high tides to float their logs while others constructed splash dams on the creeks of Swift, Clifty, Gladie, Dog Fork, and even the Red River, to create their own tides. When the dams had sufficient water to float the logs, they could be opened to send the logs roaring downstream. (See a Splash Dam Primer)

Logs were rafted together for the trip downstream and loggings crews usually rode these rafts (see River men). Danger was always present, but river men usually knew their business. However, the river still claimed an occasional victim.

According to an old time logger of the Red River Gorge the largest tree he every cut was a Yellow Poplar, measuring 48 inches in diameter and producing five logs. Yellow poplar was used often to help float heavier, denser logs such as hemlock and oak by riding these species on the top of poplar.

THE ARCANE ROCK

High on a flat ridge overlooking Swift Creek and not far from the House of Tal is a mysterious rock. The rock is sandstone, about one foot square and 8" thick with a 3" diameter hole about 6" deep. There is some resemblance to a hominy hole, except for size and the presence of a small channel cut from the hole to the outside edge of the rock. The hole is tapered from top to bottom. It appears someone went to considerable labor to produce this opening. Pictured below is the stone. Note the channels on either side.

Another mystery of Swift Creek. The general composition of the stone indicates it was carried some distance to the present site. Whether the stone was cut with this feature at the original spot or at the current location is, of course, undetermined. We will probably never know the intentions of the creative artisan who toiled over his work of producing the cavity and channel

SWIFT CREEK MYSTERY

Just below Sky Bridge in a side drain of Swift Creek, there is a small 5'x5' native stone edifice built under an overhanging cliff. The stone was laid with mortar complete with concrete floor. The door opening is about 3'x3' with wood framing on one side. There is no physical evidence of the door. The rugged terrain suggests it was no easy task to transport the material to the site. There is a faint possibility this may have been a powder house used to store dynamite caps. However, there is no evidence of another storage area for the dynamite proper.

The Pine Ridge CCC Camp, F-1 about 1933, constructed the Red River Road (now KY 715). Probably they used explosives at this time. The powder house possibility does not knit well, since the stone structure is so inaccessible.

In Sal Branch, (named for Devil Sal Sargent), a few miles downstream from Swift Creek, are two buildings one large and the other smaller, undoubtedly used to store dynamite in one and the caps in the other, during the construction of the Red River Road. They were built in a very accessible location. They are at present repositories for the trash of uncaring campers, and bare no resemblance to the stone composition on Swift Creek. They are constructed of poured reinforced concrete including the roof with thick metal doors and vents.

I first located this stone edifice in 1970. A recent visit in early 2002 showed little apparent change. After many interviews with local old-timers, I am no closer to identifying the use or date of this fabrication than I was 32 years ago. Perhaps this story will spark the memory of someone whom may bring forth knowledge of this creation in stone. There are many interesting possibilities, but scant facts upon which to base a reasonable conclusion. We will leave it at that.

THE TRINITY ROCK SHELTERS

It was my unprecedented opportunity to see the Trinity Shelters for the first time in 1973 while examining the property for appraisal purposes. The shelters were on the private property of Charles Little, who was considering selling his ownership to the U.S. Forest Service. While compiling property information, I came to the head of a hollow and decided to examine the large shelter just before me.

To my amazement, I found three large rock shelters with passageways between each. Facing almost due east, all three of the shelters indicated early occupation. The middle shelter had an abundance of cord-marked pottery shards scattered over the surface. Near the center front of the shelter was a large sandstone boulder. The light was just precise enough to reveal markings on the rock. In the amber glow of the setting sun, my wondering eyes discovered near the left side of the boulder as large inverted "V" carved deeply into the sandstone. Directly above this upside down "V" is another carving, which resembles the so-called stick man of the western states. Immediately above this was a series of inverted "v's" smaller in size in a diagonal line across the face of the rock. Near the right center was a small pecked human footprint. The backside of the rock contained smaller "v" symbols, abrading grooves and other indistinct markings. Out of all the petroglyphs I had ever seen, this was easily the most prominent. This one is, perhaps, the most significant examples rock art in the Red River Gorge.

The ancient writing could possibly represent fertility symbols. Pregnancy and birth have frequently been depicted in prehistoric rock art. This rock art could represent the symbolic man, woman and child, with the stick man being the male, the inverted "V" representing the female and the outline of the small footprint, a child.

Facing the center shelter to the right is another large shelter. It is accessible to the center shelter by traversing a small ledge beneath a waterfall. On the sandstone boulders are several deep grooved abrading areas and a nut stone at the extreme western edge with about twenty uniformly round holes. It is thought such stones were used for cracking open nuts. On the backside of the stone are three deep groves. An interesting point is that archaeologist's consensus usually holds that nut stones are common to long-term habitation areas since the size and weight of the stone used was such as to restrict transportation. Usually, accepting the presence of a nut stone at a site suggests at least some period occupied at the shelter. However, the size of the Trinity nut stone (12" x 12") makes it extremely portable and suggests the site was not a long-term habitation.

The left or southern shelter is accessible to the central shelter by a large passageway near the top of the shelter. No petroglyphs were noted in this shelter, but it was the only one projectile point and utilized flint flakes were scattered over the surface.

227

All three shelters are in pristine condition and completely undisturbed, and do not appear to have been inhabited by a family type group. Rather, it appears these shelters may have been used for a ceremonial site.

Since 1967 when Justice Douglas made his famous walk up the Red River, visitation to the Gorge has increased year by year. Visitors are exploring the backcountry as never before. Sadly, this exploration marked the end of the rock art at Trinity. In recent years, a thoughtless or uncaring camper built a fire squarely on top of this ancient manuscript, destroying for all time this record in stone. In addition, the nut stone is gone, probably carried away by relic hunters.

It was a rare experience to see Trinity in a pristine and undisturbed state under the great cathedral of overhanging rock. Surely a step beyond time, with the shelters appearing to be in the same condition as whoever left them occupied this site hundreds of years ago.

THE REEVES HOUSE

The present day Martin's Fork Trailhead covers irretrievably the former home of John and Mary Reeves. Henry Catron built the house in 1949 along with a combination stock and tobacco barn just east of the Nada Tunnel at the bottom of the grade. The house was four rooms, one story frame with two porches. It measured 22' x 25'. The barn was 39' x 43'. Henry Catron lived there for many years, before selling to John Reeves.

Pictured above is Henry Catron. The house is in background.

THE BISHOP HOUSE

A few patches of Jonquils, growing in mute testimony to a woman's touch, mark the site of the Bishop House. The house site is located just under Sky Bridge and was a two-story house with several outbuildings. Ennis Bailey in 1933 was the last occupant of the house as a tenant. The road into the property has amazing stone retaining walls. Pictured below is the farmstead when the Red River road was being constructed by CCC camp F-1, located at Pine Ridge. Note the two-story house, outbuildings and crops.

Sleepy Hollow Lodge is just out of the picture at the lower left.

THE HOUSE OF CATRON

If you should go, after reading this account, do not look for the house of Catron for it is no longer there. Over the changing seasons, only the cliffs remain the same. Look, instead, for the flat place beside the trail where Steve Catron raised his family and lived out his life under the shadow of high cliffs, farming the narrow bottoms of Martins Fork.

The house was a small board and batten, one story, typical of the time. It was built in 1922 and occupied until 1933. The site is located on the left side of Trail 221 just beyond the third creek crossing from Highway 77. You will recognize it by the Japonica bushes planted by Mamie Catron. After the family moved away, the house slowly faded into obscurity and finally succumbed to the forces of nature. Catron Arch stands nearby overlooking the house site and fields where the Catron family went about their daily tasks. Mrs. Catron raised four stalwart sons to help the family, Henry, Roy, Troy and Hugh. Steve and his sons are pictured left in a tobacco field, a cash crop for the family. Pictured below is the old house in the 1930's. Note the shake roof and corn patch.

THE JOE LEDFORD HOUSE

The Joe Ledford house on Chimney Top Creek was the most modern for the time. He acquired the property about 1900 from the Clay City Lumber and Stave Company, and by 1917 had increased his land holdings to over 4000 acres.

235

"Uncle Joe" as he was widely known married Isabelle Kilgore and built a small house on the south side of Red River near Chimney Top Creek about 1922. Set on a pier foundation, with three rooms constructed of rough lumber the house was roughly 412 sq feet. This was the original building on the tract and was later occupied for a time by White Ledford and his family as sharecroppers for Joe. After White moved away, the house was converted into a workshop.

Joe decided to construct a more modern house in 1933, hiring Sam Quinlin, Charlie Hill and Jim Tabor to do the job. As a result, the first contemporary house came to the area. The dwelling was a two-story frame structure with three rooms downstairs and three bedrooms upstairs, with a fireplace and front porch. Located near the original house, the new residence was about 1562 sq. ft. and boasted a full bath.

Joe and Isabelle (Belle) lived here for 17 years raising a family of six daughters and one son (one son died an infant) One dark stormy night with the Red River raging below, Joe turned to his wife and said, "Belle, I believe we built in the wrong place." After Joe's demise, the house stayed empty for several years. Chester and Dottie Morrison returned from California in 1959 and occupied the house until 1984 at which time the U.S. Forest Service purchased it. The original house after having been a residence for Joe and White was converted into a workshop and used in this way for many years. No vestige of the old house remains. It exists now only in the realms of the memory for kith and kin and in the imaginations of those care.

JOE

LEDFORD HOUSE
Original House 1922

Spring House

1933

**Swinging footbridge over Red River that was remodeled by
Chester Morrison in 1964. Floyd Ledford's house is in the
background.**

THE TYLER HOUSE

The Cecil Tyler house is located at the mouth of Copperas Creek within sight of the Red River. It was a wood frame structure built near a large rock. The construction date and occupants are shrouded in obscurity, but the house was still standing in 1965.

THE SWIFT CREEK FARM

The house and farm at the confluence of Red River and Swift Creek washed out in the Frozen Flood of July 5, 1939 while occupied by Henry Swango. Swango lived on this property since 1915, and built the last house. However, according to old-timers there had been a house on the same site for perhaps 100 years. One of the early predecessors of Swango was Jasper Campbell and later Kelly Sally. In addition, a Joe Amburgey had a house near Brewer's Shute. The last house on the river was at the Roundabout, but the name is lost to history.

Midway in the picture is the old log bridge across Red River. Swift Creek is near top and farmstead is on right. Jasper Campbell, Kelly Sally and Henry Swango are synonymous with Swift Creek and their names will live on as long as there are people who read this story. This picture was before the Frozen Flood, which completely washed away the buildings and crops.

PUMPKIN BOTTOM

Pumpkin Bottom was well known locally because of the size of the pumpkins grown there. It is located at a tight U-bend in the Red River just upstream from Gladie Creek. Upper Jess Branch flows into the bend from the south side. Earl Wells, of Frenchburg acquired the property and about 1940 built a weekend cabin from boards obtained from the old Gladie School. Earl sold the property to Alex Talbott, a lawyer from Louisville. It continued as a weekend retreat until David Talbott (brother) established a camping area in 1991 with the name of Pumpkin Bottom Campground. This move perpetuates the old name and insures it will not be lost to history, at least not for a little while.

Completely surrounded by National Forest with Red River frontage, it is an ideal location for this use. There is also road frontage along Kentucky Highway 715.

THE PALMER ENGLE CABIN

This cabin was built around 1968 on a steep slope on the north side of highway 715, just above the present day Sheltowee Trace Trailhead. Small white oak post with bark formed the exterior wall with cement between the post. Dimensions were about 25'x15' with a small porch. Mr. Engle used the cabin as a weekend retreat.

The U.S. Forest Service bought the property in 1982, but Engle reserved the right to use the cabin for a 10-year period. A few loose timbers mark the spot.

THE GAYHART HOUSE

The old Gayhart house was located near Wolfpen Branch high on the slope. A man made level spot is a silent reminder of the days when this house was a home. Carl Gayhart built a log style house as a retirement abode in country he had known in childhood.

The house was constructed in 1968 from native cut poplar logs stained redwood, with dimensions of about 53'x33' with a half-basement. Interior was old barn wood and wormy chestnut. The house also boasted a 7' brick fireplace. Water was from a 154' drilled well by pump. The Gayharts from 1968 to 1975 occupied the house. The U.S. Forest Service purchased the tract with house in 1979 from Kathryn Gayhart, widow of Carl. The house was removed log by log, and reassembled at another location.

RAVEN ROCK

Raven Rock is a great monolith of stone standing like a sentinel in time just off Ky Route 77. This rugged crag has watched over the valley and if words were possible, what stories could be told.

Old-timers say the name originated from the great flock of Ravens that used the rock for their roost. Stories are told about the birds blackening the sky when they flew.

In 1975, the area was developed and a steep road with hairpin turns was finally forced to the top by private enterprise. Plans were to move the old High Rock Lookout Tower to Raven Rock, but this never materialized. A bear cage, complete with a bear, was built, and a small concession stand. A hang glider ramp was also installed. Two hang glider pilots were killed in 1976 and this use was discontinued.

The U.S. Forest Service finally purchased Raven Rock.

ROSE ORCHARD

Just upstream from the Sheltowee Trace footbridge across Red River there is an area known in early days as Rose Orchard. It was here Powell Rose in the early 1850's planted an orchard of fruit trees. No trace of the orchard remains, however there is a concrete slab which marked the house of Morris Sipple. Morris obtained title to a portion of the land and built a small brick cabin in 1960 with brick from the Sipple Brick Company in Stanton, of which he was part owner. It had three rooms, and a fireplace. He lived on the property for two years, experiencing the 1962 record flood where he had to evacuate the cabin after the Red River crested at 4.3 feet above flood level. He also suffered the lost of a gun collection when someone forced his way into the cabin during his absence. He finally sold to J.O. Briggs in 1963, who used the cabin for a weekend retreat. Briggs sold to Peter Wulfeck and the cabin burned in 1976. A log rolling out of the fireplace caused the fire.
In 1977, Wulfeck sold to Hubert Pitts and Pitts sold to the U.S. Forest Service in 1980.

Rose Orchard now stands silent and the foundation of the house has covered over with vegetation. The Red River still flows nonchalantly along and the swinging bridge still spans the river. Where long ago, Powell made the area bloom, Rose Orchard is now a mere footnote in history

LEAD AND ALUM FORKS

Lead and Alum forks are two branches of Mill Seat Branch off Leatherwood Fork of Indian Creek. Mill Seat Branch was named for a sawmill located at the mouth of the stream.

Mill Seat is well known locally and it is listed by name on the USGS Map of the area. Not so well known or listed is Lead and Alum Forks. At one time, however, Lead Branch was the scene of busy activity. George W. Pitts operated a small mine here. John Henry Hatton, along with Alex and Henry Scott used to go with G.W. Pitts when they were boys to get lead. They recall a beech tree near the mine with a picture of an Indian with a gun carved on the tree.

Roy Pitts can remember two forks of Mill Seat Branch; the south fork was called Lead Branch and the north fork, Alum Branch. Roy's mother lived on a point between the forks.

This lead mine was said to be very visible and was a seam about two feet thick. I have tried, unsuccessfully, to locate this mine on at least 3 occasions. The old sawmill remains are still there as is the foundation of the house were Roy Pitt's mother lived out her childhood.

I have been unable to locate any records on the mining of Alum and have found scant evidence of any activity in Alum Fork.

As a matter of interest, John P. Hatton was the first person to be buried in the Hatton Cemetery in 1906. He married the elder daughter of George Washington Pitts -- Mary Ann. John P. was the father of John Henry Hatton who, as a boy, helped George Pitts mine the lead.

BEAVER POND

Asa T. Petit established a store or trading post around 1845 at a place called Beaver Pond. This settlement was named for a small body of water created by a beaver dam in the swampy lowlands just east of the village. When Powell County was established on the second Monday in May 1852, Beaver Pond became the county seat; however, the name was changed to Stanton which was incorporated March 9, 1854. Stanton was named for Richard H. Stanton, a member of congress from 1849 to 1855. He also served as circuit judge from 1868 to 1874, and was the author of Stanton's Revised Statues, a valuable contribution to Kentucky law.

He lived in Maysville, and there is no record of his ever having resided in Stanton.

An 1852 record indicated that in Powell County there were 363 white males over 21, 49 slaves over age 16 and 602 children between the ages of 5 and 16. In 1860, the population of the county was 2,257, with 59 living in Stanton. The 1870 population of Stanton was 73, and it 1895 it stood at 200.

Court House
Stanton, Ky.

256

DARK HOLLOW

Dark Hollow is located on Route 77 immediately before the junction with Route 715. It is a short narrow drainage with a small bottom near the mouth just before it empties into Red River. In this bottom, a few loose rocks mark the old house of Dorothy Sexton. It was here that George Sexton died after being shot by Taylor Coldiron. This is the story as told to me.

At the present day junction of Route 77 and 715, where an old barn now stands, a sorghum mill was set up in the early 1930's. Taylor Coldiron was making the sorghum when George Sexton walked up unaware he was nearing his last days on this earth. After a while, fresh trouble developed between Sexton and Coldiron. The problem had been brewing for some time. For whatever reason, Coldiron drew a 38 revolver from his person that contained only one bullet, and shot Sexton through the right side. Sexton's sister, Dorothy, lived just below this junction in Dark Hollow. Sexton, fatally wounded walked to the house of his sister and was in great agony during the two days it took him to die, unattended by any doctor. The place became known as Dark Hollow, a name that has endured to this day.

Dark Hollow Arches are located high on the cliff overlooking the little bottom and serve as reminders of the frailty of life, while standing like a stone cenotaph to the memory of past and yet to be tragedies.

WARRIOR FORK

The Red River, once named Warrior Fork, was well known at a very early date. Dr Thomas Walker crossed the Red and explored up the north fork, calling it "The Big Creek." Christopher Gist traveled along the river in 1751 and declared it was "the roughest country he had even seen."

It is unclear how the stream became known as the Red River. Daniel Boone in his early explorations of Kentucky relates of having crossed a river named Red. It is possible the origin of Red River's name could be associated with the numerous natural iron seeps common throughout the area.

It is a matter of record that in 1791 William Suddith, a land surveyor, came to the Red River apparently in the employment of Eli Cleveland and John Morton. The records show in that year these two men entered 1483 acres on two Treasury Warrants (no.15.132 and 12.128) on a branch of Red River and including an old camp (John Swift?).

It appears, however, that Daniel Boone was more interested in Red River, we find him returning repeatedly. In 1782, he entered two tracts of land in the Kentucky Records. One tract contained 1000 acres and the other 500 acres. Both tracts were situated on Red River.

The Red River is about 90 miles long and technically does not meet the established
standards for a true river. Beginning as a small rivulet that may be easily crossed, at the foot of Town Flats, the approximate corner of Wolfe, Morgan, Magoffin and Breathitt Counties, the Red meanders through the rolling countryside of Hazel Green as a calm and peaceful stream. Then plunges into a ridge of the Daniel Boone National Forest and winds its sinuous way through vertical canyon walls in isolation for 10 tortuous miles, emerging at the Red River Bridge at the Wolfe/Menifee County line. The next 8 miles parallels Kentucky 715 and is a boulder-strewn waterway but relatively calm. After leaving the National Forest, it becomes a quiet stream again before flowing into the Kentucky River near Boonsboro.

The Red has three forks, north, south and middle. The north is the main fork and the south is the shortest. The major part of the river is within three counties, Powell, Menifee and Wolfe.

In 1993, a section of the Red was designated as a National Wild and Scenic River, the first stream in Kentucky honored with this title.

TRACING THE RED RIVER

Natural influences on the landscape of the Cumberland Plateau in Kentucky created a unique geologic condition, the Red River Gorge. The gorge, because of its shape, weather patterns and soils provides a rare variety of plants and animals not found other places. The river valley was inhabited by the earliest humans and provided a settlement area for the generations that followed. The thread that binds together and touches each of the stories of geology, ecology and human influence in the gorge follows the PATH OF A RIVER.

After the process of sedimentary rock formation and uplifting, a plateau existed with a maze of irregularly winding narrow-crested ridges and deep narrow valleys.
Over time, the river and streams began to sculpt out some of the valleys and form deep fissures in the land. Today the small, quiet Red River flows through a narrow valley of steep cliffs and bizarre rock formations, keeping the secret of its powerful history when, along with other natural forces, it was a RIVER CARVING OUT A LANDSCAPE.

River valleys provide many of the things needed by living beings, such as food, water, power and often good soil for farming. River valleys are often the easiest way for travel through a dense forest with steep slopes. Since the river valleys could provide an easy pathway and a good place for people to settle, ancient man and early explorers of the Red River Gorge followed the RIVER PATHWAY.

Resources within the Red River Gorge interested people in the 1800's who wanted to start new industries. The timber on the steep slopes attracted people from the north to acquire land began logging. Communities were established along the river and creeks to provide labor for the timber industry. As settlements grew along the riverbanks, and its strong spring currents became important for logging operations the Red became the RIVER OF OPPORTUNITY.

Gladie Creek, near the Red River, became a thriving logging community. After the logging declined in the gorge, the loggers left the Gladie community. New settlers moved in and farmed, growing crops that flourished in the valley. Artifacts and buildings that remain from the period tell the story of early logging and farming communities and the lives of those who chose to be part of the RIVER SETTLEMENT.

With the end of the logging industry and the great depression, owners of land in the gorge area began to sell their property to the U.S. Government for National Forest purposes. As the approach to forestland changed, management and conservation became the focus. The Red River Gorge today provides recreation, education and a place of awe-inspiring views and solitude. The public plays an important role as a partner in protection, thus ensuring future use and enjoyment by becoming personally involved in the PRESERVATION OF THE RIVER RESOURCES.

LOG RAFTING THE RED RIVER

During the early logging days the logs were driven on the smaller streams with grappling hooks from the bank as they drifted singly with the current. When the river was reached most of the logs were formed into rafts and guided down by oarsman. On the Red River only half rafts could navigate. The rafts averaged sixty feet long and from ten to fifteen feet wide containing about eight thousand feet of timber.

The logs were arranged so their length formed the breadth of the raft and bound together by long poles, held by iron "chain-dogs." Usually there were two men to a raft with log oars. The rafts averaged about four miles per hour and could not navigate at night. Pay for the rafters was about two dollars per day.

In the early logging years, species of trees were selected that would float readily, namely walnut, yellow poplar, ash and hemlock. Needless to say, it was not long before the supply of high-grade trees was consumed.

The log rafts were floated to Clay City, which had two planning mills, one of the nation's largest sawmills, a spoke factory and several tie yards.

FULL CIRCLE

For a moment in time, oil was king when the sputtering engines that supplied power to the jacks could be heard in almost every hollow of the oil fields. Perhaps the great towns envisioned in early development never materialized, but for a period the iron works, timber and oil played an important role in the history of the region. Unfortunately, these resources played out and the dreams of glory for the Red River Valley are only footnotes in history.

With the opening of the Mountain Parkway in 1961, a new wave of people flocked to the Red River Gorge. They come to see essentially the same things that attracted early man, who was certainly awed by the geological art, just as visitors are today. Early man camped and lived under the vast cathedral of overhanging rock, and using, as some believe, the great natural arches as places of worship or ceremonies.

Therefore, in a sense, we have come full circle. The same things that attracted early man is bringing back visitors in ever increasing numbers, creating a new industry—Tourism. Many, reminiscent of the ancients, are seeking a regeneration of life through the transcendent of natural phenomenon.

FROM TIMBER TO OIL

As logging declined and slowly faded, crude oil or Black Gold helped fill the void of employment for local people. In the years from 1916 through 1965, there were 19 million barrels of oil pumped in Estill County alone.

The Wood Oil Company was one of the successful companies in the area. Others include South Penn Company, Petroleum Exploration and Swiss Oil. Swiss developed into a giant corporation with holdings throughout the world-- the Ashland Oil and Refining Company.

 During the early oil boom, the country was replete with oil pump jacks operated by a system of shackle rods from a central powerhouse. The powerhouse engine used natural gas from the wells and turned a large wheel connected to the rods, which ran sometimes for miles. The shackle rods were about 20 feet long and had threaded ends for connecting together. A powerhouse could handle several jacks pulled by these rods. As the wheel revolved, the rods pulled on the jacks providing the pumping action necessary to remove the oil.

Later, electricity was used to operate the pump jacks, enabling the pumps to kick off and on automatically reducing the need for manpower.

According to records Dean Pieratt was issued the first lease for oil and gas on the Cumberland National Forest in 1949.

SPLASH DAMS

During the early logging of the Red River Gorge a series of so-called splash dams were built at intervals along the different creeks to add volume to the stream. These dams were made of long tree trunks staked to one another and sealed with rocks and mud. Each obstruction backed up the water to a depth of six or eight feet. The logs were piled in the stream bed in stretches between the dams, and when the spring rains filled the river the dams were either blown up by explosives or, if the revolving type, by knocking out pin holding the gate. This unleashed a torrent of water and the logs in the channel were picked up and hurled on in the stream to the next dam. This dam, too, was blasted or the pin tapped out and the logs continued in this manner until they reached the river.

The stationary type dams were used in the smaller streams such as Silver mine Branch, where it was anticipated the logging could be done in a short time. The revolving type could be used repeatedly and were built on the larger streams such as Glade and Swift Creek. There were also several revolving dams in the Red River.

The remains of one revolving dam were visible on Swift Creek, until a flood removed the last vestige a few years ago. There is an excellent model of a revolving dam on display at the Gladie Creek Historic Site.

RAILROAD TIE INDUSTRY

At one time hewing railroad ties was a thriving source of income in the Red River Gorge for the local folks. The building of railroad tracks required enormous quantities of crossties. In fact, one mile of track needed from 2600 to 3300 crossties depending on the size of tie and the service the road must render.

Standard lengths of narrow gauge ties are 5, 5 ½, 6, 6 ½, and 7 feet. Standard-gauge ties are 8, 8 ½, and 9 feet long. Crossties were hand hewed in the early days and untreated, but are now sawed and treated with a preservative.

White oak appeared to be the best species for untreated ties having an average life span of eleven years, followed closely by chestnut with a span of 10

years. Hickory and yellow poplar 5 years and sycamore 3 years. In the early days of the railroads, the crossties were made by hand in the woods. The trees were felled, cut into the proper lengths, and hewed out with the broadax.

Young trees were used for the best grade of ties. As a rule, hewed ties were manufactured in small lots by the landowner. Some companies bought the timber and engaged their own labor.

Later, an increasing number of ties were manufactured in the sawmills owned by the lumber companies. Here, smaller and less perfect trees can be used than in handwork. However, hewed ties could still compete with those made in the mills on account of their superior endurance, which is due to the selected timber and their smoother faces, which shed water.

THE TANBARK INDUSTRY

The stripping of trees for tanbark was in important industry to areas of the Red River Gorge accessible to the railroad. At one time only chestnut oak was used, but later hemlock and chestnut trees were in demand. All grades and sizes of chestnut above five inches in diameter were used, as well as the limbs and tops.

The trees were sometimes peeled while standing, cut into four-foot lengths, piled and air-dried before sale. The bark was stacked by the cord. A cord of dry bark weighed about a ton. Usually, when the tree was to be cut, two girdling rings were chopped around the butt of the tree, one near the ground and the other one four feet or higher. The bark was split vertically, and pried off with axes or spuds. This first "coil" of bark was removed from the tree to prevent loss of valuable bark when the tree was felled. After the tree was down, girdling rings were cut at four-foot intervals along the bole and the remaining bark removed.

Prior to the introduction of the vacuum pan for concentrating tanning extractions, bark was the principal raw material used in tanneries. It was customary for tanners to buy bark, store it under cover, and then as required, make extracts by leaching crushed bark in hot water.

LOADING TANBARK ON RAILROAD FLATCAR

The peeling season usually begins in May and ends in August. The ease of peeling is influenced by weather conditions. The bark will adhere, or "bind down," on cold days and on hot dry days.

FROM IRON TO TIMBER

A bloomery forge was established at the Great North Bend of the Red River near present day Clay City in 1787. Its founder was Steven Collins who produced what may have been the first iron in Kentucky.

The first furnace established in this area was in 1807 by William Smith, near Clay City and named the Red River Iron Works. The furnace operated about 23 years from 1807 until 1830. In 1832, it was moved and rebuilt as Estill Furnace.

The three furnaces in the area during their working span produced 126,122 tons of iron clearing 41,620 acres. John Mason and J.L.Wheeler built Cottage Furnace in 1854, Estill Furnace was built by Mason, Wheeler and Samuel Jackson in 1832 and Fitchburg by Sam Worthley (designed by Fred Fitch) in 1869.

The great financial panic of 1873, caused by over speculation in western railroads helped along the demise of the furnaces. Since most of the iron production went for railroad car wheels, production slowed down due to the lack of a market. Other factors causing a decline was the furnace's were very near or beyond the economical limits of hauling timber or iron ore. The final blow, however, was the discovery of the iron ore beds in Alabama. Since this ore was of better quality and easily accessible, this clanged the death knell of the furnaces.

The old furnace's had their day. Where once smoke and fire belched out of the stone chimney, grass and moss have taken root. The shouts of the ironworkers have given away to the cries of birds and insects. The furnaces faded into long years of obscurity, awaking as a modern day attraction.

The iron industry had declined by 1880, but a renewed interest in timber began prompting the Kentucky Union Railway to construct the first railroad into the Red River area. However, the cost of building a railroad through such rough terrain and other problems forced the KU into insolvency. A new corporation, The Lexington and Eastern Railway (L&E) succeed the old KU in 1894.

In 1887 first large sawmill was erected on the north bank of Red River adjacent to the present town of Clay City. Isaac Norcross and J.M. Thomas owned it. In1889 the Kentucky Union assembled at Clay City what was to become the second largest sawmill complex in the nation. It had a daily capacity of 200,000 feet. Logs from the Red River Gorge were floated to these early mills a distance of about 20 miles. Again KU experienced financial difficulty and the mill was purchased by the Swan Day Lumber Company in 1898. This company owned about 8000 acres in the gorge.

The Dana Lumber Company, builder or the Nada Tunnel, constructed a standard gauge railroad through this tunnel to the Red River drainage beyond. The company purchased about 2500 acres located in Grays, Fish Trap, Auxier and Edward's Branches. This property had been virtually unlogged by the earlier timber companies.

In 1914 The Dana sawmill at Nada was completely destroyed by fire. Dana never rebuilt but leased its entire acreage and sold all its appurtenances to the Broadhead-Garrett Lumber Company, who rebuilt the mill. Between 1914 and 1920, Broadhead-Garret launched the most massive timbering effort in the history of the gorge. By using an ingenious system of splash dams, logs were floated to the mouth of Chimney Top Creek, where they were caught and held by the "Great Log Boom." A log loader would hoist the logs into cars ready to be trained to the Nada mill. After the logs were sawed into lumber they were stacked, air-dried and finally loaded on the main line railroad to be exported to distant markets.

 By 1920 the timber had been harvested and Broadhead-Garrett ceased operations, thus closing the last major logging effort in the Gorge. In 1932 the U.S. Government began buying these large cut over tracts for national forest purposes. In 1937 this purchased land was named the Cumberland National Forest, a designation enduring until 1966 when it was proclaimed the Daniel Boone National Forest. Currently, the forest spans over 650,000 acres.

THE GLADIE CREEK BRIDGE

The original Gladie Creek Bridge was a log structure spanning Gladie Creek at or near the same point as the new bridge in place today. For the day and time, it was a masterpiece of engineering and construction.

It is unclear just when the log bridge was constructed, but old-timers state it washed out in the Frozen Flood of July 5, 1939. It was replaced by a treated pole cribbing, uprights, and concrete surface by the WPA in 1940. This bridge served well until 1999 when the current bridge, a concrete and stone combination that blends well into the environment, replaced it.

The original bridge was a classic. The foundation was native log cribbing forming a "V" at the upstream end to split the flow of the stream in high water. The surface of the bridge was logs placed perpendicular to the stream flow in corduroy fashion with pole uprights and railings. The structure was fastened together with long eight-inch spikes. Some of these spikes are on display at Gladie Historic Site.

NICKELL GROCERY

At the junction of K77 and 715 there existed for many years a country store known at that time as Nickell's Grocery. The store was owned and operated by Henry and Maggie Nickell, and was opened after Henry had worked numerous years on the log railroad and public works. It was the only store in the gorge area at the time.

Henry established the store about 1949 and continued in business for over a quarter century, before moving to Frenchburg where he died.

He watched from this vantage point as the visitors leaped from a few vehicles per day to an astonishing half-million in the early 1970's.

The store at the junction of KY 77 and 715 with Henry and Maggie

Henry Nickel is first one standing on the log loader of Dana Lumber Company next to Bob McNabb. Randell Harter is on the Dana engine. Corb and Dave Lawson are on loader.

THE EARLY IRON INDUSTRY

Three old charcoal burning iron furnaces still stand as a silent reminder of the all but forgotten iron industry in this area. Several factors were essential for the location of an iron furnace—an adequate supply of iron ore, thickly forested lands, and a good supply of limestone. Having all of these in abundance, Kentucky was at one time the center of the iron industry in the United States. The time was from about 1790 to the late 1870's, an era when more than 100 iron were in operation in Kentucky alone.

The ordinary furnace was a big pyramid of sandstone, varying in size, but typically, 30 feet square at the base and from 25 to 35 feet high. There was no effort made to smooth the three or four foot square blocks of sandstone that were used to build the structure. They were left in a rough state and placed without benefit of mortar. Due

to the intense heat, mortar would have been useless.

An exception to these usual structures is the Fitchburg Furnace. This furnace was constructed of cut stone, smoothed and shaped, with a cornice at the top. It was also, being a double furnace, considerable larger in width and height. It was at the time reputed to be the largest in the world. The furnaces were named Chandler and Blackstone after the stockholders.

As might be expected, the manufacture of pig iron required huge amounts of timber to furnish the charcoal. It has been estimated it required three tons of iron ore, and the clearing of three-tenths acre for the charcoal to make one ton of iron. Hence, acres and acres of timber were cut down. Cottage Furnace had a producing life of 25 years manufacturing 34,170 tons of iron and clearing an estimated 11,270 acres to produce the charcoal.
Estill furnace 56 years and 25,040 acres and finally Fitchburg with a life of 5 years and clearing 5,300 acres. The economical limits of hauling charcoal were soon reached.

The furnaces had their day than began a swift decline during the great financial panic of 1873, and after the discovery of rich iron ore beds in Alabama. Since the iron ore in this district was too small in quantity and too far away from the railroads, competition was impractical, clanging the death bell for the old furnaces.

Therefore, these furnaces representing an investment of more than a million dollars closed down toward the end of the nineteenth century. One by one, the fires in the old furnaces flickered out, never to blaze again, thus writing the final entry in the journal of the iron industry in Kentucky.

For an account of how charcoal and pig iron were made, see "A History of the Fitchburg Furnace."

Cottage Furnace   1854-1879
Estill Furnace   1832-1888
Fitchburg Furnace 1869-1874

THE SAM RHULE HOUSE

If you should drive along Route 715 a mile or so from the intersection of Route 77, you will see on your left a small rock quarry. This site conceals the former location of the house of Rhule. The house was built by Sam Rhule in the 1950's, enduring until 1998 when the house, which had fallen into ruin, was demolished and rock quarried from the area to provide fill material for the new Gladie Creek Bridge.

Sam Rhule was an oil and water well driller, known locally as one of the best. He was a resident of Tarr Ridge in Menifee County.

The Sam Rhule house exists now only in the realms of memory as does so many former houses in the Red River Gorge. These photographs and stories insure they will not be lost to history.

WHITE-HAIRED GOLDENROD IN THE RED RIVER GORGE

E. Lucy Braun first described White-Haired Goldenrod (Solidago Albopilosa) in 1942. She listed the plant as occurring in sandstone rock houses of the Basal Pottsville formation in Menifee and Powell Counties. (An annotated catalog of spermatophytes of Kentucky, pg. 139).

Paul Higgins in a 1970 Thesis entitled "A preliminary Study of the Vascular Flora of the Red River Gorge, Kentucky," lists the Solidago Albopilosa as occurring on upper slopes in Powell County.

Mary E. Wharton and Roger W. Barbour in 1971 described Solidago as "A species which grows in dense shade under overhanging sandstone-conglomerate cliffs in the Cumberland Plateau. It is urgent that it be protected. (The Wildflowers and Ferns of Kentucky, pg 248).

In 1972, Don F. Fig, active in recording Solidago colonies since 1964, launched a massive campaign to inventory sites and was later joined in this effort by Johnny Varner and Johnny Faulkner. Results were the finding of not only large additional populations, but also a sizeable concentration in Wolfe County where previously this species was listed only in Powell and Menifee Counties.

In 1974 The Final Environmental Statement for the Red River Lake Project, list Solidago as occurring in Powell County under rock shelters on the upper slopes. (COE, Final Environmental Statement, pg. 96).

A 1975 report by Clifford C, Amundsen (The Red River Gorge Geological Area, Evaluation for Consideration as a National

Landmark) states, "The most unique species in the Red River Gorge is Solidago Albopilosa. This is a woodland species of Goldenrod that has been found in no other place. This discovery was made by Dr. E. Lucy Braun in 1942." Pg. 15.

A 1983 publication "A Report on Some Rare, Threatened or Endangered Forest Related Vascular plants of the South", volume II, assigns four pages to Solidago. Pg. 54.

In 1985, all district records were turned over to Mark Evans of the Kentucky Nature Preserve Commission.

It has been 80 years since Dr. E. Lucy Braum discovered the White-Haired Goldenrod in the summer of 1942 in Powell and Menifee Counties. Protection measures are at last underway.

THE STAVE INDUSTRY

The making of staves is of comparatively short duration since it is based on the oak and disappears with the exhaustion of that tree. Split staves are usually made in small lots after the more valuable timber has been marketed as saw logs. Trees are felled, sawed into stave lengths, than split into billets, which by means of the hearting – ax is chopped out from the sapwood, and left as a round block. Billets are split from the blocks with a frow and wooden maul and dressed. When finished, the staves are stacked in pile or ricks for about three months of seasoning before shipment.

In 1906, split staves of average length (twenty-six to fifty-four inches) delivered at the railroad brought from twenty-five to seventy-five dollars per thousand. Whiskey staves must be clear of sap one inch on heart, and they average a thirty-six inch length. They require the best grade of white oak.

Long unshaven shingles an inch thick and three feet long are split with the frow from smaller trees. These are used locally as roofing and only the surplus is shipped.

Squared billets were split from hickory and sent the mills at Clay City where they finished into spokes and sent to wagon factories. Finally, yet importantly, is the riving of pickets with frow and maul used for the old stake and rider fences characteristic of this area.

STAKE AND RIDER FENCE

THE SHOOTING OF POWELL ROSE

An act to the establish the county of Wolfe July 1, 1860 mentions the mouth of Wolfpen Creek where the same empties into the north fork of Red River, below Powel Rose's old farm. It is interesting to note that in 1860 the farm was considered "old." Powell Rose was born June 8, 1802 and was shot to death on January 10, 1854 at his home in the shadow of Chimney Rock. He was the founder of the Boat Yard at the mouth of Chimney Top Creek, a farmer, logger and county official. In 1852, the Powell County Court appointed Powell Rose, among others, as viewers; to view the ground along which a road is proposed to be conducted.

This is a story as told to me by an old time resident in a taped interview at his home, about the demise of Powell Rose:

Powell Rose and another local settler named Pitts had "bad blood" between them since an earlier disagreement involving a bear trap. One day after all this happened, Pitts stopped by the Rose house. It was about dinnertime, and Rose invited him to stay and eat. Pitts accepted and as was the custom removed his pistol, an old cap and ball, from his pocket and placed it on the bed. This was a large family and by tradition, the men would eat first. Rose would not eat at the first table, but Pitts did. While Pitts was eating, Rose removed the pistol from the bed, took out the cap and spit in the powder, rending the gun useless, and placed it back on the bed. When Rose came in to eat, Pitts was suspicious and went to check his gun. When he saw what had happened, he put in a new cap, fresh powder and laid the gun back down on the bed.

Meanwhile, Rose had been drinking heavily and looked on the bed where the gun was located to see if it was still there. When Pitt's came into the room, Rose lunged at him with a knife, thinking Pitt's gun was harmless. Pitts picked up the supposedly harmless gun from the bed and shot Powell Rose dead.

Apparently, Rose believed the gun to be harmless or else thought he could finish Pitts before he could reach the gun. Powell Rose had a daughter who was the only witness to this tragedy. She swore every word the truth, so that cleared Pitts.

Powell Rose is buried near his home at the mouth of Chimney Top Creek in the Shadow of Chimney Rock. If Chimney Rock could speak, this convoluted monolith could weave many stories about Powell Rose. From the time, a Black Panther leaped onto the hindquarters of his horse while on a trip to Swiftville, to the witnessing of the falling boulders, that now surround the old house site, bounding from the cliff face.

THE SWIFT CREEK STORE

About 1971, Tyra Enterprise constructed a country store and campground on Swift Creek. This marked the first time a store was in operation in this section of the Gorge. While it lasted, the store was a picturesque edifice with friendly keepers.
For one reason or another, the campground and store were abandoned in 1975 and fell into disrepair and decay. Vandals ravaged the structures so all that remains are concrete slabs as attestation

that something was once here. The property passed into federal ownership in 1998. The building was a one story frame, board and batten on a concrete slab. It contained an 8'x9' living quarters for the keeper. Power was propane tank that operated the heating and lighting system. It was also wired for electrical in the event it became available. Outside dimensions were 20' x 40' with a composition shingle roof. A gravel parking lot covered 100' x 35'.

The store was operated by the owner as part of a campground business that included a shower/laundry concrete block building 26' x'50' on a concrete slab. In addition, a water treatment tank and reservoir with sand filter served the building.

Although in operation less than four years, the Country Store and Campground had their day than faded away into oblivion, to be revived from time to time through conversation and photographs.

PINE RIDGE CCC TRAGEDY

On Saturday morning, July 23, 1938 a CCC truck loaded with
25 enrollees were on
their way to work when a serious accident occurred on the Sky
Bridge road two miles from Pine Ridge.

As the CCC truck with crew was driving towards Sky Bridge
they met a half-ton pickup truck rounding a sharp turn in the
road. The CCC truck driver pulled over to avoid a collision and
the vehicle turned over and rolled down a steep incline.

Matthew Nis of Cincinnati, Ohio was killed.
James Mullins of Ashland, Kentucky suffered a broken leg and
two fractures.
John O'Neal of Louisville, Kentucky sustained a broken leg and
bruises
Albert P. Vogel, Cincinnati, Ohio injured left shoulder.
Wm. Curl, Louisville, Kentucky endured a broken back.
Nathan Taulbee of Taulbee, Kentucky injured arms and leg.
C.E. Reynolds of Louisville, Kentucky injured leg.
Millard Pelfrey of Campton, Kentucky injured hip and suffered
broken rib.

Many of the other CCC truck passengers sustained injuries such
as cuts and bruises.

PINE RIDGE PICNIC SHELTER

The Pine Ridge Picnic Shelter was constructed in 1935 at a cost of $5000, while still a part of the Red River Ranger District. The shelter was log, 168 x 34 feet with a flagstone floor, rock fireplace and chestnut shake roof. The structure was demolished in 1960 to accommodate the Mountain Parkway. Pictured below is the shelter in its halcyon days.

The shelter served the public well in the early days of the Red River District, which was headquartered at Mt. Sterling, Kentucky and contained both of what is now the Morehead and Stanton Ranger Districts. In 1954 the headquarters was moved to Morehead Kentucky, but still called the Red River Ranger District. In 1960 the Red River District was divided into two districts, Morehead and Stanton. The first Ranger Station at Stanton was a part of the old Ashland Service Station across from Hearne Funeral Home. The second was the old chiropractor's office on Route 15 near the present day Assembly of God Church. Finally, in 1968 a new office was completed on 3 ½ acres, across from the old IGA store on Cider Hill. The station is still at this location today.

THE WOLFPEN CULVERT

The Wolfpen culvert was a part of the construction of the Red River Road and is a signature in stone work. Started in 1936 by CCC Camp F-9, the culvert was one of three on the road, but by far the largest and most imposing. The others were at Copperas Creek and Duncan Branch. Ed Halcomb was the foreman on the job and the estimated cost was $5800.

The Wolfpen culvert is approximately 58 feet long and has double 10 x10 openings with curved wing walls. Constructed of native sandstone quarried locally, the keystone style includes a stone paved floor completed in 1937. This massive work of sandstone is a priceless structure standing like a giant cenotaph to the work of CCC Camp F-9, at Bowen, Ky.

Downstream view of culvert under construction (circa 1937) showing keystone arches and superb stonework.

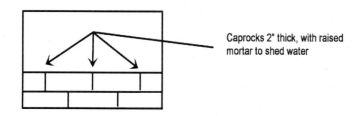

Caprocks 2" thick, with raised mortar to shed water

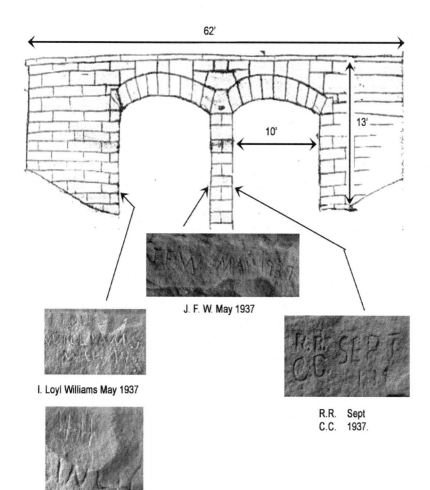

62'

10'

13'

J. F. W. May 1937

I. Loyl Williams May 1937

R.R.   Sept
C.C.   1937.

H.H. Inch

SWIFT SILVER MINE

What the Golden Fleece was to Jason and his Argonauts, so is the fabled lost silver mine of John Swift to residents and visitors alike of eastern Kentucky.

Down through the past two centuries, the legend of this mine where silver could be "picked up in chunks" has persisted. Despite intensive searching by expert and novice alike, nothing even remotely approaching such a rich lode has ever been found.

John Swift, an English adventurer and convicted counterfeiter, was supposed to have learned of the mine from a French youth by the name of Alfred Munday, while in the Carolinas. Munday supposedly learned of the mine while held captive by the Indians.

According to a "Journal" which Swift left with a Mrs. Renfro at Bean Station in Tennessee, he made at least eight trips into eastern Kentucky during the period of 1761 to 1769, smelted a considerable amount of silver, and transported it out by horseback. Copies of this "Journal" exist today, much altered, and the tempting story continues to intrigue people.

Another story is that Swift was a former pirate who came into this region from Alexandria, Virginia about 1706, bringing with him a vast treasure in silver articles plundered from ships on the eastern seaboard. Here these silver articles were melted and cast into bars, and in some cases, money. Returning east with a supply of silver ingots, Swift conveniently accounted for his wealth with tales of a rich silver mine in the far away mountains of Kentucky.

Although geologists state earth composition of this region is not the type that contains silver in ˙ paying amounts, belief to the contrary still remains. So the search, like the stories, still goes on. The lost silver mine of John Swift is a dream that never dies.